StyleCity

# NEW YORK

StyleCity

# NEW YORK

## THIRD EDITION

**With over 400 color photographs and 8 maps**

Thames & Hudson

# Contents

## Street Wise

## Style Traveler

Series concept and editor: Lucas Dietrich
Research and texts: Alice Twemlow, Joshua David Stein
Jacket and book design: Grade Design Consultants, London
Original design concept: The Senate
Maps: Peter Bull

Specially commissioned photography by
Ingrid Rasmussen, Anthony Webb, Yoko Inoue
and Peter Dawson

The **StyleCity** series is a completely independent guide.

Every effort has been made to ensure that the
information in this book is as up-to-date and as
accurate as possible at the time of going to press,
but some details are liable to change.

Second edition published in 2005 in paperback in the
United States of America by Thames & Hudson Inc.,
500 Fifth Avenue, New York, New York 10110

thamesandhudsonusa.com

Third edition 2009

Library of Congress Catalog Card Number 2009902031

ISBN  978-0-500-21024-6

Printed in China by C & C Offset Printing Co Ltd

## How to Use This Guide

The book features two principal sections: **Street Wise** and **Style Traveler**.

**Street Wise**, which is arranged by neighborhood, features areas that can be covered in a day (and night) on foot and includes a variety of locations – cafés, shops, restaurants, museums, performance spaces, bars – that capture local flavor or are lesser-known destinations.

The establishments in the **Style Traveler** section represent the city's best and most characteristic locations – "worth a detour" – and feature hotels (**sleep**), restaurants (**eat**), cafés and bars (**drink**), boutiques and shops (**shop**) and getaways (**retreat**).

Each location is shown as a circled number on the relevant neighborhood map, which is intended to provide a rough idea of location and proximity to major sights and landmarks rather than precise position. Locations in each neighborhood are presented sequentially by map number. Each entry in the **Style Traveler** has two numbers: the top one refers to the page number of the neighborhood map on which it appears; the second number is its location.

For example, the visitor might begin by selecting a hotel from the **Style Traveler** section. Upon arrival, **Street Wise** might lead him to the best joint for coffee before guiding him to a house-museum nearby. After lunch he might go to find a special jewelry store listed in the **shop** section. For a memorable dining experience, he might consult his neighborhood section to find the nearest restaurant cross-referenced to **eat** in **Style Traveler**.

Street addresses are given in each entry, and complete information – including email and web addresses – is listed in the alphabetical **contact** section. Travel and contact details for the destinations in **retreat** are given at the end of **contact**.

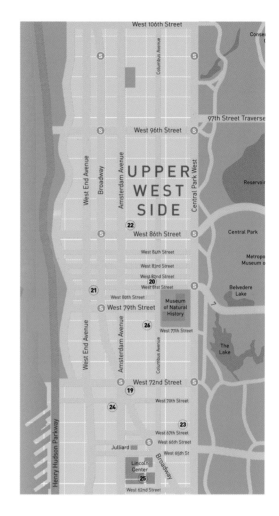

Legend

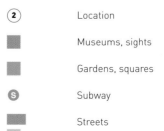

| | |
|---|---|
| **2** | Location |
| | Museums, sights |
| | Gardens, squares |
| S | Subway |
| | Streets |

# NEW YORK

"There are eight million stories in the Naked City," says the narrator in Jules Dassin's great New York film-noir masterpiece, *The Naked City*. That was in 1948. Now with the population of the New York metropolitan area hovering around the 18,000,000 mark, there are ten million and counting. Only a few of them can be heard distinctly, but it is this great chorus that gives New York City its distinctive sonic backdrop and vitality. The true New York Philharmonic isn't just found in Lincoln Center; the entire city is an orchestra, from the avian honk of taxis and stockbrokers to the tonal crescendo of an argument in Chinatown, the timpani rumble of businessmen making deals to the quiet sweep of autumn leaves across Central Park's Sheep Meadow. The entire Lower East Side is one big brass section, the lush Upper East Side the woodwinds, and Central Park the seat of sweet, singing strings.

Unlike other unbound metropolises, New York is an island. It doesn't spread out like London or Paris. Water, not walls, demarcates its boundaries: the East River on the East Side and the Hudson on the West. So all the players and all their instruments jumble atop one another. Bars get pushed into basements or up into penthouses. Cuisines get fused. Three hundred square miles of humanity reach 1,250 feet up into the sky (the Empire State Building) and 160 feet deep beneath the asphalt (the 1/9 train at 191st Street). And nearly each foot is occupied by human endeavor, a voice struggling to be heard through the chaos. It is this struggle to be heard over competing instruments that drives New York endlessly forward and toward the next big thing. It is like that now, and has been since the Dutch East India Company first stumbled upon the island's green pastures in 1624.

In no more eloquent way do voices from history speak to us than through architecture. From the great neoclassical fortification of Castle Clinton on Manhattan's southern tip and the handsome if showy mansions of industrialists like Henry Clay Frick and Andrew Carnegie, to the Beaux-Arts touches of Bemelmans Bar (p. 82) and tiled chambers of Grand Central Station (p. 66), voices transcribed in granite and marble call out to the attentive visitor. The ability to transform the city, as well as the city itself over time, has drawn many of the world's best architects and designers to New York: Frederick Law Olmsted, who transformed a riotous bramble into one of the world's most beautiful parks; Frank Lloyd Wright, whose modernist snail of the

Guggenheim Museum (p. 85) rises on the east side of Olmsted's Central Park; Mies van der Rohe's Seagram Building; and the crown of New York's internationalist modernism, the Le Corbusier-, Oscar Niemeyer-, Sir Howard Robertson-designed UN Headquarters (p. 68).

Though styles have shifted, the sweeping architectural ambitions of the city haven't ceased. Renzo Piano's glass-and-steel New York Times Building (p. 71), the strangely stacked cubes of Kazuyo Sejima and Ryue Nishizawa's New Museum (p. 55), and the terracotta expanse of the newly redesigned Museum of Arts and Design (p. 74) all testify to the continued architectural vitality of the city. But design is not remanded to the monumental. Great style is found nearly everywhere, on every scale, from the antique vials and greenish glow of Apotheke (p. 158) to the tractor-seat stools of Brooklyn's Fette Sau (p. 139). From the inseams of clothing and the imaginative entrées of restaurants, there is little that hasn't been considered.

The gravitational pull of New York has drawn all those desirous of being a big fish in the biggest pond. There are a lot of superlatives here: biggest, best, most. The need to distinguish oneself and the ample market for almost anything has spawned a teeming agora of new ideas and products. One wonders if the experimental theater of The Kitchen (p. 41), the cashmere-covered bricks at Project No. 8 (p. 165), the Victorian charm of the Bowery Hotel (p. 130), or Wylie Dufresne's molecular gastronomic riffs (see WD-50; p. 58) could exist and flourish in such close proximity anywhere else than in a city whose citizens are consumed by production and defined by their consumption. The sheer heft of New York's population creates an economy of scale by which each fancy and kink of the human mind may be fully explored and afforded the opportunity to blossom. Nearly every niche is represented, for these ten million stories have ten million narrators and millions more characters. If you can make it here, the saying goes, you can make it anywhere.

The economic downturn has quelled, momentarily, some of New York's outspoken bravado. But the diminuendo is neither permanent nor fatal. The brash consumption of Wall Street is a mere pitter-patter now, and it would be untrue to say that its change of fortunes hasn't cast a pall over the city. But it is during these times of quiet that often unheard voices make themselves known. Out of the rubble of the East Village and the Lower East Side of the early 1990s grew a thriving arts scene. Williamsburg, once barren, now isn't. This guide is an invitation to listen to the city and conduct your own New York Philharmonic.

# Street Wise

Tribeca • Chinatown • Little Italy • Nolita • SoHo • NoHo •
Chelsea • Meatpacking District • West Village • Gramercy
Park • East Village • Lower East Side • Lower Manhattan •
Midtown • Upper East Side • Upper West Side • Harlem •
Williamsburg • Long Island City • Dumbo • Park Slope •

Tribeca
Chinatown
Little Italy
Nolita
SoHo
NoHo

New York is a city of transitioning neighborhoods, and nowhere is their ebb and flow more apparent than in the acronym-happy villages below and around Houston Street. In the late 1970s the once-decaying industrial buildings of Tribeca (Triangle Below Canal) began to be converted into residential lofts by artists who were deserting SoHo in droves because of rising rents. Over the following two decades, A-listers – Robert De Niro among them – snapped up gargantuan lofts in late 19th-century cast-iron buildings and the area's population increased exponentially. Chic eateries soon followed, and today the neighborhood is completely gentrified, with a host of furniture and architectural salvage stores and a sprinkling of fashion boutiques.

The sudden shift from one community to the next within the space of a block is continually startling. One minute you are walking in a sea of red plastic bags, the unofficial logos of Chinatown's food markets, and the next you are hit by the smell of salami and coffee wafting out of one of the remaining Italian delis. There are few places in Little Italy that still give a sense of its storied past: the Ravenite Social Club on Mulberry Street, for example, where celebrity don John Gotti held court from the mid-1980s until his arrest in 1990, is now a handbag and accessories store. But there are some that still give you a whiff, albeit a friendlier one, of what it used to be like on these mean streets. The district known as Nolita (North of Little Italy) is the area with the highest concentration of new boutiques and Europhile cafés. These businesses sprang up in the late 1990s and, in a heartbeat, displaced the local Sicilian community. The term 'Nolita' describes a fashionable lifestyle as much as it does a geographical area.

SoHo was the center of New York's art scene from the 1970s until the mid-1990s when chain stores started to move in, raising the rents, ousting old stalwarts and pushing the more interesting stores and galleries to areas outside its perimeter. Although SoHo's heyday has long since passed, the beauty of the area's distinctive cast-iron buildings with their zigzag fire escapes, the bottle-glass sidewalks that allow light into storage vaults below, the streets of Belgian brick and traces of Jean-Michel Basquiat's graffiti heritage here and there can cause you to forget for a second the rude invasion of global brands. And sandwiched between the strip-mall of lower Broadway, East Houston Street and the East Village is an unspoiled oasis called NoHo, with Bond Street as its primary spokes-street. The ground floors of the historic loft buildings with their façades of marble, cast iron, limestone and terracotta have largely been returned to their original usage as retail stores.

This grandly proportioned space, once the site of the Mercantile Exchange, was remodeled in 1989 by owners Bill Katz and Karen Waltuck into an elegant, airy dining room. Seemingly immune to the vagaries of fashion influencing its Tribeca neighbors, Chanterelle has retained the same classic interior ever since. Its features include magnificent floral arrangements, and widely spaced tables set simply with white linen and china. Large windows are half covered with sheer curtains, and the reception area walls are hung with artworks by the likes of Cindy Sherman and Cy Twombly. The menu, which changes every four weeks, features hearty French dishes such as beef fillet with oysters and oyster sauce.

Twelve-foot (4-meter) half-moon windows, low Guastavino-style vaulted ceilings hung with chandeliers, and walls painted blood red provide a suitably dramatic setting for chef David Bouley's culinary spectacles. The witty tasting menu starts with a porcini flan, accompanied by Dungeness crab and black-truffle dashi, and ends, four courses later, with an amaretto flan with caramelized banana, white-coffee mousse and amaretto ice cream.

Nestled in the middle of a busy intersection in Tribeca is an unexpected green triangle of calm and beauty. New York's second oldest public park has the active support of locals, who look after its historical importance and keep it fresh with new plantings. Lying at the heart of Tribeca, it also provides a good vantage point from which to observe the richly detailed brick buildings that surround it.

This store, on the ground floor of a cast-iron building, carries Issey Miyake's womens- and menswear lines, including his experimental A-POC clothing range, and all of the accompanying accessories and fragrances. Frank Gehry collaborated with the architecture firm G Tects to create the titanium wave that dominates the store's interior. Many of the techniques used for the Bilbao Guggenheim were applied here to create the billows and curves of the metallic structure that offsets the Japanese designer's convention-busting wares.

Elusive Brit art dealer Gavin Brown chooses to position Enterprise just outside the fashionable concentration of galleries. As soon as other spaces invaded his original south-of-Chelsea territory, he upped sticks and moved even further down Manhattan to an out-of-the-way location at the bottom end of the West Village. But with a continually fresh roster of YBAs and American up-and-comers including Urs Fischer, Martin Creed, Laura Owens, Elizabeth Peyton, and Spencer Sweeney (an artist and proprietor of Santos Party House; p. 18), collectors and critics are never far behind.

A good selection of interesting and reasonably priced beers and international wines can be found at this enduring and unaffected bar. Dark and candlelit in winter, breezy and spilling out onto the sidewalk in summer, the laid-back, homey ambience is perpetuated by the combination of owner Craig Weiss's vision, an unpretentious staff with good taste in independent music, and a local crowd happy to escape the tyranny of the velvet rope.

NOODLES IN CHINATOWN

### 11 Great NY Noodletown

28 1/2 Bowery

Like a dumpling, the charms of Great NY Noodletown are hidden by a humdrum exterior. This restaurant at the base of the Manhattan Bridge looks like any other Chinatown hole-in-the-wall, but the Cantonese food draws everyone from city officials to local residents and gourmet snobs. The noodles, especially those found in the wonton soup, are the some of the best in the city, but it's the duck – crispy and succulent – that makes a visit worth the invariably long waits and the brusque service.

BOOGIE NIGHTS

### 12 Santos Party House

96 Lafayette Street

New York doesn't want for clubs or bars, but Santos Party House is a much-needed nightlife addition. Opened in 2008 by artist Spencer Sweeney (see Gavin Brown's Enterprise; p. 17) and musician Andrew W.K., the space weds art, music and a full bar in a way that has been missing from the city scene lately. The programming is wildly varied and includes everything from Punk Rock Pillow Fights to sessions featuring jam band Endless Boogie. Most refreshingly, nobody seems to come here to be seen. Though the place is undoubtedly a hot spot and the clientele well connected, the crowd is here to dance.

FASHION COLLABORATION

### 13 Opening Ceremony

33 Howard Street

Opening Ceremony is as much an experiment as it is bicoastal avant-garde boutique. Humberto Leon and Carol Lim operate the space along the Olympic principles laid out by Pierre de Coubertin, founder of the International Olympic Committee, in 1896. Each year Leon and Lim pit American designers against those chosen from an annually rotating cast of countries. The aim is to collaborate as well as curate, most recently with a line of menswear by indie actress Chloë Sevigny, combining these efforts with the work of such designers as Proenza Schouler and Mary Ping, as well as vintage pieces, art zines and the discreet charm of the hip bourgeoisie.

PEOPLE-WATCHING AND COFFEE

### 14 Caffé Roma

150

STREET ARCHITECTURE

### 15 Storefront for Art and Architecture

97 Kenmare Street

Designed by Steven Holl and Vito Acconci in 1993, this gallery space for architectural thought and practice bursts beyond its tiny slice-of-pie footprint. The irregularly rectilinear plates in the concrete-board façade revolve on vertical and horizontal pivots, so they can flip open to the street, making the space an exercise in mutable architecture.

A RELIC FROM LITTLE ITALY

### 16 Albanese Meats & Poultry

238 Elizabeth Street

Bounded by the Bowery to the east, Lafayette to the west, Houston to the north and overlapping with Little Italy to the south is the province known as Nolita. Mott, Mulberry and Elizabeth Streets, in particular, are lined with meticulously curated boutiques that open and close like so many pretty butterflies. Albanese Meats & Poultry, sitting resiliently in a street now recast by trendsetting young retailers, is an original relic from a time when the area was a Sicilian enclave.

CAFÉ CULTURE

### 17 Café Gitane

146

VELVET UNDERGROUND

### 18 I Heart

163

NOT FOR PEASANTS

### 19 Peasant Wine Bar

194 Elizabeth Street

Nolita's Elizabeth Street is a strip of unremitting hipness, but if you stumble down the unmarked stairs looking for a brief respite from the glamour, you'll be disappointed. Instead, you'll find stylish quaffers sitting along rough-hewn benches and on rickety shabby-chic chairs illuminated only by candelabra, sipping wines from the extensive list and nibbling on classics like the award-winning thin-crust pizza from the upstairs restaurant's kitchen. Though Peasant Wine Bar is still a scene, it's cozier and more low-key than the neighboring Café Gitane (p. 146) – more like a campfire for beautiful people.

NOLITA SOCIAL CLUB
**23  Café Habana**
17 Prince Street

If you can get (and keep) a table at this buzzing corner luncheonette, use it as your Nolita model-watching HQ. The nuevo-Mexican/Cuban menu offers a range of spicy dishes, but the grilled corncob rolled in grated cotija cheese and chilli powder and sprinkled with lime juice is the one the regulars go for.

TRENDS FOR MEN
**25  Unis**
226 Elizabeth Street

Hand-painted, banana-leaf wallpaper lines the walls (you can buy rolls of it at the desk), the music is just right, and there is a stylish range of casual T-shirts, anoraks and trousers in this tasty morsel of a menswear boutique.

ART FOR EVERYONE
**26  Jen Bekman**
6 Spring Street

This tiny gallery has an unapologetically commercial and populist bent. Established in 2003 by the former employee of an Internet startup, the storefront space features new and up-and-coming photographers. Bekman's ethos of "art for everyone" is best embodied in programs like 20X200, an ever-revolving selection of photographs printed in editions of 200 and sold for $20 online. But Bekman is not just an online entity. She's also a talented curator and puts on exhibitions – like "De/Construction," featuring paintings by Sarah McKenzie – that seem much larger than the small space in which they're contained.

FEEL THE BURN
**27  The New York Shaving Company**
202b Elizabeth Street

After years of razor burn, John Scala decided to open his own barber shop in a tiny Nolita storefront. Hirsute patrons recline on antique barbers' chairs and are treated to the "ultimate shave," a half-hour depilatory extravaganza featuring a procession of homemade elixirs and balms, much pomp, and many hot towels. Scala took great care in turning the former video store into a true gentlemen's salon, but there are modern touches here, too. Patrons are offered cappuccinos and snifters of cognac before and after each shave.

VINTAGE INSPIRATION
**30  Lyell**
173 Elizabeth Street

This small dress shop run by designer Emma Fletcher carries her own line of feminine dresses, velvet jackets and flouncy silk-chiffon blouses, alongside her picks of vintage clothes, shoes and jewelry. Fletcher uses a stamped-tin ceiling and authentic 1940s wallpaper to create an evocative yet understated setting, in contrast to many of her glitzy, glammed-up neighbors.

A TASTE OF MEXICO
**31  La Esquina**
114 Kenmare Street

Serge Becker, the man behind La Esquina, is a master of detournement. He's taken the classic taqueria look and converted it into a hipster food emporium. First there's the Corner, the counter-service lunch spot. Behind that, there's the sit-down version with an expanded menu (including one of the best fish tacos this side of the Rio Grande). But the real secret is the basement brasserie. The über-hip restaurant is reached after a *Goodfellas*-like trek through the kitchen. The large dining area and bar is full of old wood and candelabras, like the set of an Antonio Banderas shoot-em-up peopled with extras cool enough to know the reservation number. Now that includes you.

CIVILIZED REFINEMENT

**32  Greenwich Hotel**

116

IT'S A MAN'S WORLD

**33  Jack Spade**

170

COUTURE MAGAZINE'S GALLERY

**34  Visionaire**

11 Mercer Street

This small gallery puts on curated shows and reflects the inspiration and process behind the irregularly appearing and limited-edition *Visionaire* album. Conceived by Stephan Gan, Cecilia Dean and James Kaliardos, this couture version of a regular magazine has taken various forms and involved luminaries from the worlds of fashion, art and design. A recent issue, entitled *Sport*, featured twelve Lacoste T-shirts with images from creatives like Pedro Almodóvar, Karl Lagerfield, Phil Poynter and David Byrne of the Talking Heads. Each set – which came with three shirts – runs to $250. For the less affluent, there's *V* magazine, a large format fashion mag for $6.50.

SOHO BRASSERIE EPITOMIZED

**35  Balthazar**

80 Spring Street

Even if you don't have time for a multistory iced-shellfish platter at this infamous SoHo brasserie, make sure you do, at the very least, breeze in and out, either to pick up a croissant in the adjoining pint-sized patisserie or for a bowl of steaming café au lait in the bar area. Worn red leather banquettes, age-spotted mirrors and nicotine-stained paint were used to create an already aged French bistro look in this airy 180-table space. "I didn't have in mind a particular restaurant in France that I was trying to imitate," says owner Keith McNally, "but there are bits and experiences of various restaurants that have stuck with me." Balthazar is one of those SoHo landmarks – others being the Prada store (p. 170), Dean & Deluca, the window of Pleats, Please, the bathroom at Bar 89 – that you just have to see; they are part of the deal.

FISH BAIT

**36  Lure Fish Bar**

146

SUBLIME JEWELRY

**37  Ted Muehling**

27 Howard Street

Pay homage to craftsmanship and beauty at this minimal store dissembling as a gallery space. Muehling's sculptural jewelry is inspired by organic forms such as shells, rocks, coral, eggs and berries. The simple shapes are exquisitely rendered in brushed gold or finely hammered metal. His delicate ceramic work is manufactured at the Nymphenburg porcelain factory in Germany, and all of the pieces are beautifully displayed in tall glass cases.

CURATORIAL EXPERIMENTATION

**38  Artists Space**

38 Greene Street, 3rd Floor

A pioneer in the alternative-space movement, Artists Space was founded in 1972 as a non-profit institution supporting contemporary artists. Today the gallery is one of the few exhibition spaces to exploit the dynamic interchange between practice that involves design, video, new media, performance, architecture, and art. In its thirty-seven-year history, Artists Space has presented the work of over 5,000 emerging artists.

GOING APE

**39  A Bathing Ape**

91 Greene Street

An unmarked location, no website, and carefully controlled quantities of stock are some of the more unusual techniques Japanese designer and sometime DJ Nigo uses to promote Bathing Ape. His candy-hued sneakers, influenced by old-school hip hop and worn by contemporary rappers Jay-Z, Cassidy and Pharrell, among others, are the main attractions of his new minimalist store as they rotate on a conveyor belt in the window. Inside, you'll find a pared-down assortment of urban streetwear, accessories and limited-edition toys.

**40  Donald Judd House**

101 Spring Street

This five-story cast-iron building, dating to 1870 and located on the northeast corner of Spring and Mercer Streets, was purchased in 1968 by the archdeacon of minimalism, furniture maker and artist, Donald Judd, and is now managed by Judd's estate. You can look through the ground-floor windows and see some of Judd's pieces, as well as the work of Carl Andre and Dan Flavin, two of the artists whose work he collected. While the inaccessibility of the building's interior may be frustrating, it's a lot easier than traveling to Marfa, Texas, the town that Judd transformed into an art installation.

ANARCHY IN TOYLAND

**41  Kidrobot**

118 Prince Street

Catering to all your urban vinyl, action figure, and plush toy needs, this emporium for grown-up kids contains glass case-loads of cute and bad ass characters like Smorkin' Hate Dunny (a Pepto-Bismol pink rabbit with a five o'clock shadow and cigarette) and Babo the Uglydoll by artists David Horvath and Sun-Min Kim. When yet another Statue of Liberty snow globe just won't do, take home a toy by a New York City graffiti artist such as Quik, Dalek, Tristan, Lase NYC, Filth or Dr. Revolt.

ART PLAYGROUND

**42  Deitch Projects**

- 76 Grand Street
- 18 Wooster Street

Some of the most ambitious presentations of emerging art, design, and music take place in Jeffrey Deitch's two SoHo project spaces. With an A-list of international artists and friends at Deitch's beck and call – Kehinde Wiley, street artist Swoon, Ryan McGinness and Mariko Mori among them – the experimental gallery owner is able to assemble shows that enchant even the most jaded of New York's "artgentsia." The Wooster Street space, the size of a garage, hosts occasional site-specific installations and performances – for a recent show, "Be Kind Rewind," Michel Gondry (the director of the film of the same name) converted the space into a New Jersey video store, a junk yard, a doctor's office, and more. The more intimate Grand Street gallery is home to a regular program of exhibits.

RETRO-FUTURO DESIGN

**43  Alessi**

130 Greene Street

When the iconic Italian design company Alessi opened up its sleek flagship SoHo store in 2006, they contracted Asymptote's Hani Rashid and Lise Anne Couture to come up with a fitting interior. The result is stunning. The long, angular space is bound by strips of light; the front half of the store, girded on one side by a sleek counter and on the other by low benches and ottomans, is actually a café, while the back half, taken up by Alessi's playful silver saucers and utensils, ends in a mirrored wall so that the whole store starts again. The shop – a winner of the American Institute of Architects' design award – is a necessary destination, whether you're in the market for an espresso, an espresso demitasse, or just good design.

FORMER SPEAKEASY

**44  Fanelli's**

94 Prince Street

Fanelli's has been serving food and drink in inimitable, no-nonsense style since 1847. This genuine bar, incongruous in its central SoHo location, has managed to weather a fashion tempest that has swept along Prince Street, leaving bland chain stores in its desultory wake. Bob the bartender is a retired prizefighter, and a wall of original boxing photographs and portraits from the early 1900s pay tribute to the pugilist's art.

HAUTE ARCHITECTURE

**45  Prada**

TWIN PEAKS IN SOHO

**46  Merc Bar**

151 Mercer Street

With a colorful Vacation in your hand (the bar's signature drink, available in pink, green or blue), you are ready to lounge on a brocaded ottoman or the long cowhide couch in this classic SoHo watering hole. The fabulousness of the rustic but comfortable mountain lodge-style bar is nicely faded, like a pair of well-worn jeans. Restaurateur John McDonald also owns Lure Fish Bar (p. 146), in SoHo, and the Marc Newson-designed Lever House Restaurant (p. 143) in Midtown, as well as being editor and publisher of the design, fashion and food rag, *City NY*, a stylish magazine that McDonald sees as the American answer to *Wallpaper\**.

VIVA ITALIANA
**47  Joe's Dairy**
156 Sullivan Street

Though only a small storefront, Joe's Dairy is a crowd-pleaser. Typography lovers will be seduced by the obviously handcut sign from the 1920s advertising Lattecini Freschi, and gourmands can't help but fall in love with the homemade mozzarella, which, thankfully, dates back only to the morning. Anthony Campanelli, who took over from the original Joe forty years ago, makes his cheese fresh five days a week. Joe's Dairy, which sells all sorts of old-school Italian foodstuffs, is more than just a cheese store or a food stop. It's a reminder that SoHo had a strong Italian community long before the Prada store (p. 170) arrived.

HALF-MILE OF BRASS RODS
**48  The Broken Kilometer**
393 West Broadway

Viewing American artist Walter De Maria's 1979 installation of 500 polished brass rods, precisely placed in five parallel rows, is a strangely ethereal experience. His Earth Room of 1977 (see below) is located a few blocks uptown on Wooster Street.

FRAGRANCE LABORATORY
**49  Helmut Lang Parfumerie**
81 Greene Street

Gluckman Mayner's store for Helmut Lang provides a suitably hard-edged laboratory setting for the designer's fragrance line. The narrow entry is emphasized by an LED installation by Jenny Holzer that runs the length of the interior along the top of an enameled steel wall.

FASHION SUPERMARKET
**50  Kirna Zabête**

164

NATURAL SANCTUARY
**51  The New York Earth Room**
141 Wooster Street

Created in 1977 by Walter De Maria (see The Broken Kilometer; above), this pastoral sculpture consists of one SoHo loft and 250 cubic yards (190 cubic meters) of topsoil. This is the only Earth Room project still in existence; De Maria's previous installations in Munich (1968) and Darmstadt (1974) have since been dismantled.

AN APPLE A DAY
**52  Apple Store**
103 Prince Street

Need to check your email? Avoid the charges at passé cyber cafés and pop into the Apple Store, where you can log on at one of Apple's latest computers. Aside from the array of state-of-the-art digital cameras, iPods and Mac accessories in this gleaming white space designed by Bohlin Cywinski Jackson and Ronette Riley, there is a "Genius Bar" at which to get your technical questions answered and an amphitheater where workshops and demonstrations are held.

DESIGN MUSEUM
**53  Moss**

167

DELICATE RUSTICITY
**54  Delicatessen**
54 Prince Street

When the last of the old Nolita delis, a place called Buffa's Coffee Shop, met its match in 2006, it didn't take long for the space to be reinvented. Delicatessen, which opened to much fanfare in 2007, is a stylish riff on an old meme: comfort food in a warm room. The award-winning interior by Anurag Nema incorporates sleek steel-and-glass garage doors that roll up during the summer and rustic wood planks on the walls harvested from Vermont barns, while the food by Franklin Becker is a sophisticated reworking of old classics. But it's safe to say that the model citizens who make up the clientele are substantially more hip than the old locals who used to enjoy a 75¢ coffee at Buffa's.

BATHING BEAUTY
**55  Red Flower**
13 Prince Street

Owner Yael Alkalay, former creative director of Shiseido, is behind this shop devoted to bathtime pleasures. Yuzu mimosa sea algae wash, gingergrass bamboo scrub, and wild cherry blossom rice buff are just three of the seven signature Red Flower products created to reflect the ritual of Japanese bathing.

CAMOUFLAGED STORE
## 56 Nom de Guerre
640 Broadway, Lower Level

Hidden beneath a Swatch store on Broadway is a collection of rare, discontinued and imported clothing and sneakers, assembled by Isa Saalabi and Holly Harnsongkram of Williamsburg boutique ISA. The army theme continues throughout the bunker-like interior in the form of khaki-draped changing rooms and gunmetal shelving. Labels include such local talents as Yoko Devereaux, Tess Giberson, Asfour and Spawning.

LOUIS SULLIVAN IN NEW YORK
## 57 Bayard Building
65 Bleecker Street

The only building in New York designed by American master architect Louis Sullivan, a fifteen-story bright-white edifice, is best viewed from the corner of Houston and Crosby Streets. The use of terracotta cladding over the building's structural steel frame is a hallmark of the Chicago School, an architectural style closely associated with Sullivan.

VERDANT OASIS
## 58 Liz Christy Garden
East Houston Street and Bowery

Thanks to the work of activist Liz Christy, the Green Guerillas and a thirty-strong team of volunteers, NoHo's visitors and residents have a surprisingly ample oasis of oxygen emanating from the northeastern bank of Houston Street. The Liz Christy Garden, founded in 1973 as the first community garden in New York, boasts a pond with fish and red-eared slider turtles, a beehive and a wildflower habitat, a grape arbor, a grove of weeping birch trees and hundreds of varieties of flowering perennials.

DOMESTIC HISTORY PRESERVED
## 59 Merchant's House Museum
29 East 4th Street

This 1832 row house is among the finest surviving examples of the late Federal and Greek Revival architecture of the period. This former residence of prosperous merchant Seabury Tredwell and his large family is situated in what was then a fashionable "uptown" district of the city. Three floors of this fascinating home are available for viewing. And, if asked, the knowledgeable docents will explain the details of the formal parlors that feature identical black-and-gold marble mantelpieces, an Ionic double-column screen and mahogany pocket doors that separate the rooms. And don't forget the back garden, an otherworldly retreat, restored to its 19th-century glory.

ACCESSORY PALACE
## 60 Bond 07
168

FOLLOW YOUR NOSE
## 61 Bond No. 9
9 Bond Street

There are many smells in New York, but relatively few that you would want to wear. But the olfactory concoctions created by founder and nose Laurice Rahme are ambrosial. The logo, inspired by subway tokens of yore, and the distinctive, broad-shouldered bottle scream New York, but the scents speak for themselves. Madison Soirée is an ultra-feminine perfume for ladies who lunch, while New Haarlem is sultrier with coffee and patchouli notes.

WILD-AT-HEART PERFORMANCES
## 62 Joe's Pub
425 Lafayette Street

This contemporary take on the cabaret lounge serves up avant-garde music like jazz guitarist Doug Wamble's exploration of William Faulkner, and theatrical performances including Justin Bond's gender-bending cabaret. The nightly after-hours DJ parties are for a crowd of nocturnal hipsters who have outgrown punk and aren't jaded enough yet to not care about sincere works of art.

DJS' DELIGHT
## 63 Other Music
15 East 4th Street

Other Music is Manhattan's hands-down best record store, with its stock of unclassifiable musical genres unconventionally (and amusingly) categorized as In, Out, Electronica, La Decadanse, Krautrock, Psychedelia, and Then. Tickets to most of the city's hottest gigs can be purchased here. Look out for in-store performances from the likes of Conor Oberst, Vampire Weekend, Jim O'Rourke, and Stephen Merritt of the Magnetic Fields.

CHURCH OF VODKA
## 64 Temple Bar
159

PAPER CORPORATION

GAGOSIAN GALLERY

# Chelsea
# Meatpacking District
# West Village

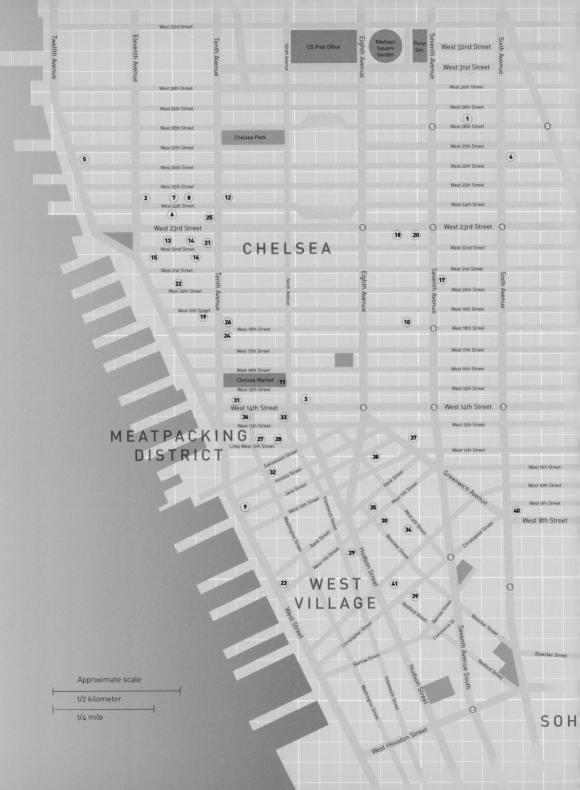

Chelsea takes its name from the estate of Captain Thomas Clarke who, in 1750, retired to the then-rural area after winning glory in the French and Indian Wars. The estate itself had been named for London's Chelsea Hospital for retired soldiers. By the 1850s, Clarke's grandson had developed the neighborhood into a proto-suburb of elegant brownstones on tree-lined streets. When landfill was used to extend the waterfront by three avenues, the newly claimed land was taken over by piers, garages and warehouses, and tenements to house immigrant workers. And thus a division between the eastern residential and western industrial parts of Chelsea arose. Apart from the addition of huge apartment buildings, including the 1,670-unit London Terrace in 1930 and public housing projects in the 1960s, there are many blocks in the eastern swathe that are little changed since the 19th century. The industrial section, however, has undergone an enormous revitalization since the caravan of blue-chip art galleries began to arrive from SoHo in the mid-1990s.

Today the "white cube" area enclosed by Tenth and Eleventh Avenues and 20th and 26th Streets has the highest concentration of contemporary art galleries in the world, as well as fine examples of converted-use buildings, such as the Chelsea Market (p. 36) in an old Nabisco factory. Chelsea's vibrant gay community is reflected in the character of many of the restaurants, clubs and stores that stay open late into the night. To the south and west is the Meatpacking District, a wholesale meat market since the 1930s. Until the late 1990s, when the designer boutiques, start-ups and restaurants began to invade its lockers, its cobbled streets were the daytime hangout for brawny meat packers and the nighttime catwalks of transsexual prostitutes. Now there are fewer than thirty meat dealers operating in the area, and one gets the feeling that it may be only a matter of time before they disappear altogether.

Continue your wanderings south through the off-grid streets of the West Village, which, with its low Federal and Greek Revival row houses, plentiful parks and specialist stores, truly feels like a village. Once the stomping ground of rebellious artists, bohemians and intellectuals, and later the seedbed of numerous contemporary social movements like feminism and gay liberation, the West Village is now a commercialized tourist trap. Stick to its western reaches — the narrow streets that crisscross Hudson and Bleecker — for your explorations. Development of the riverside beyond the West Side Highway has led to the conversion of its decaying piers — which until recently were used by late-night cruisers — into verdant leisure parks, and a pathway now runs the western length of Lower Manhattan, to the delight of cyclists, rollerbladers and joggers.

STREET EFFLORESCENCE

### 1 Flower District

West 28th Street, between Sixth and Seventh Avenues

You can catch the scent of this stretch of 28th Street well before you reach it. Ever since the 1870s – when flowers became popular for display in upper-class residences – this area has been home to New York's plant and floral wholesalers. Today it is the smallest and most threatened of the city's few remaining single-trade districts. The vendors, specializing in orchids, silk flowers, topiary trees or florists' supplies, use the sidewalks as an extension of their display space, so that they become a patchwork of huge crates of variegated tulips and planters of wheatgrass. Even if you don't have time to enter the tiny stores and jostle with party planners and floral designers, merely walking down the street between the hours of 4:30am and noon is an olfactory and visual experience that should not be missed.

MONUMENTAL WORKS

### 2 Gagosian Gallery

555 West 24th Street

Heavyweight dealer Larry Gagosian consummated the art world's newfound love for Chelsea when, in 2000, he moved his gallery from SoHo to West 24th Street. With 20,000 square feet (1,860 square meters) of industrial space to play in, Gagosian's is the largest commercial art gallery in Chelsea. One of the first shows to exploit the monumental proportions of the Gluckman Mayner-designed space was Richard Serra's *Torqued Ellipses* in 1999. Since then, Gagosian has consistently shown work from names as large as Serra's monolith sculptures: Andy Warhol, Alec Soth, Cy Twombly, Carsten Holler and Takashi Murakami, to name a few.

LITTLE SHOE

### 3 Scarpetta

355 West 14th Street

Some of the best of New York's restaurants are found in townhouses, including Dovetail (p. 86), French standby Aureole, and Bobo in the West Village. Scarpetta, housed in an 1840s Greek Revival townhouse which has been given a makeover by designer S. Russell Groves, is a welcome addition to the genre. Chef Scott Conant's spaghetti al pomodoro bursts with Roma tomatoes, pepper-infused olive oil, basil, homemade pasta, and the knowledge gleaned from having run the kitchens of two highly regarded restaurants: L'Impero and Alto.

**4 Annex Antiques Fair and Flea Market**
Sixth Avenue, between 24th and 26th Streets

For an intriguing archaeological dig into Americana's substrata – with furniture, vintage clothing and jewelry, paintings and quirky antiques particularly well represented – look no further than this collection of weekend flea and antiques markets, centered around 26th Street and Sixth Avenue. Come at sunrise for the choice goods and at dusk for the bargains. Hot dog vendors hover in the vicinity, but a more pleasant refreshment break can be found at the Antique Café at 65 West 26th Street.

MODERNE CREATIVE CENTER
**5 Starrett Lehigh Building**
601 West 26th Street

This colossal industrial building, built in 1931 by Russell G. Cory, Walter M. Cory and Yasuo Matsui, might almost be a streamlined ocean liner grounded on the bank of the Hudson River. Its brick spandrels and continuous wraparound windows elicit vistas up and down the Hudson and make this a modernist landmark well worth the trek out west. A few years ago the building saw an influx, followed by a rapid outflux, of dot-commers. Among the current inhabitants are Martha Stewart's studio, the late Jay Chiat's Screaming Media, several noteworthy art galleries and a rare bookstore. An elevator, originally used to hoist freight-train cars and now used by FedEx trucks, can be found at the building's core.

BEETHOVEN IN CHELSEA
**6 Gladstone Gallery**
• 515 West 24th Street
• 530 West 21st Street

Barbara Gladstone's caravan of high-powered contemporary artists has hopscotched from Midtown to SoHo before landing in Chelsea in 1996. Since starting her gallery in 1980 on West 57th Street, Gladstone has made her name in spotting now-huge artists like Matthew Barney and Gerhard Richter. Her current roster includes the duo Allora & Calzadilla, whose recent exhibit, "Stop, Repair, Prepare: Variations on Ode to Joy," consisted of a piano with a person-sized hole in the soundboard, in which various pianists stood while performing the fourth variation of Beethoven's Ninth Symphony.

ART DISTRICT PIONEER
**7 Matthew Marks Gallery**
523 West 24th Street

Matthew Marks was the Chelsea art district's primary pioneer. In 1994 he moved his gallery from an apartment space on Madison Avenue to an ambulance garage on a windswept and – apart from the cab drivers washing their cars – deserted 22nd Street. Now he shares with Barbara Gladstone (see left) a disused knife factory on 24th Street, and his artists include Nan Goldin, Gary Hume, Fischli/Weiss, Roni Horn and Andreas Gursky.

MINIMAL GALLERY
**8 Luhring Augustine**
531 West 24th Street

This minimalist space – another Gluckman design – was founded in 1985 by co-owners Lawrence R. Luhring and Roland J. Augustine. Check out the imposing back office where the big deals are made. The gallery's critical monographic exhibitions of Marcel Duchamp, Gerhard Richter and Donald Judd put it firmly on the map. And it continues to show German painters like Gunther Forg and Sigmar Polke, along with international photographers and conceptual artists – Sophie Calle, Robert Gober and Rachel Whiteread among them.

HOTEL ON THE HIGH SEAS
**9 The Jane**
124

UPTOWN BARGAINS DOWNTOWN
**10 Barneys Co-op**
162

WHOLESALE FINE FOOD
**11 Chelsea Market**
75 Ninth Avenue

Originally the Nabisco factory and the birthplace of America's best-loved cookie, the Oreo, this building is today a buzzing market complex. Its street block-sized interior houses a variety of specialty food shops, including Amy's Bread and the Ronnybrook Dairy that double as wholesale and retail outlets. Architect Jeff Vandeberg and developer Irwin Cohen have created a playful atmosphere using features from the original factory, such as gears, pipes and machines, as sculptural details along the central concourse. But if you want a higher-end lunch, Morimoto and Buddakan are located in the same building.

After an evening of hopping from gallery opening to gallery opening, curators, artists and dealers alike flock to the Chelsea art scene's favorite feeding ground. The delicious Tuscan food satisfies the body, leaving the mind to ponder such critical issues as the future of landscape painting in contemporary art. Fifteen wines are offered by the glass to accompany dishes such as bocconcini of fresh mozzarella, tuna carpaccio and bresaola with arugula. At lunchtime ask for a table on the patio seating area, one of the finest outdoor oases in town.

Printed Matter is the world's largest non-profit institution dedicated to the promotion of publications made by artists in a book-like format. After many years of operation in SoHo, Printed Matter moved its stock – limited-edition artworks, books, magazines and objects that blur both the definitions of, and the boundaries between, books and art – to new, larger premises in the heart of the Chelsea art district. While the store still maintains its roots in traditional artists' books by the likes of Sol LeWitt, Lawrence Weiner, and Ed Ruscha, it has recently begun to explore more contemporary interpretations of the genre, including video tapes, CD-ROMS and multiples, along with exhibition catalogs and monographs.

ART AND ARCHITECTURE COLLIDE

**14 Max Protetch Gallery**

511 West 22nd Street

In addition to casting his net beyond the conventional boundary of art practice, Max Protetch specializes in drawings by architects. Since 1978, when he moved his gallery from Washington to New York, he has shown the work of Robert Venturi, Michael Graves, Zaha Hadid, Frank Gehry and Tadao Ando. The gallery represents the estates of Frank Lloyd Wright and Buckminster Fuller, and also has on its books such artists as Iñigo Manglano-Ovalle, Oliver Herring, David Reed, Thomas Nozkowski, Byron Kim and João Penalva. A 2003 show by Manglano-Ovalle filled the gallery with a fiberglass and titanium alloy foil scale model of a 20-mile-long (30-kilometer) cumulonimbus cloud entitled *Cloud Prototype No. 1.*

INSTALLATION ART DESTINATION

**15 DIA Center for the Arts**

535 West 22nd Street

Take the elevator to the roof of this Gluckman Mayner-renovated building and start your visit with a bitter espresso in the small café you'll find there. Enter Dan Graham's Rooftop Urban Park Project glass sculpture and rotate 360 degrees, taking in the view of boats coming down the Hudson River and the immediate skyline of water towers and local gallerists' rooftop terraces. Then descend the staircase lined with Dan Flavin's fluorescent light pieces, floor by floor, viewing the large, long-running exhibitions of works by such artists as Lawrence Weiner, Ann Hamilton and Fred Sandback. Leave some time for browsing the playful ground-level bookstore with its tiled floor in candy colors designed by Cuban artist Jorge Pardo.

## 16 Comme des Garçons
520 West 22nd Street

With an entrance that looks like the gangplank to an alien spacecraft, it's hard to resist the lure of this veritable gallery of a shop, an appropriate environment for the structural architectonics of Rei Kawakubo's cult line of clothing. Future Systems, the experimental British firm that designed the space in 1998, kept the building's 19th-century façade intact and focused instead on creating the asymmetric tubular entrance made from aluminum.

CLEAN AND SIMPLE
## 17 Malin + Goetz
177 Seventh Avenue

New York duo Matthew Malin and Andrew Goetz created a unisex skincare system that consists of just six items: one cleanser and one moisturizer each for face, hair and body. Craig Konyk's minimalist store design set the tone for the packaging, designed by New York firm 2x4 in a limited palette of blue, green, red and all-caps Helvetica. And lest the whole thing sound too sharp and clean, the shop dogs Bob and Junior are on hand, lounging in the window, to mess things up a bit.

ECCENTRIC TAPAS
## 18 El Quijote
226 West 23rd Street

This sixty-year-old Spanish restaurant is the cafeteria – albeit one serving lobster and paella – for the eccentric guests of the Hotel Chelsea (p. 128). But the reason to linger here is the bar, which provides old-fashioned drinks, a comprehensive catalog of Quijote figurines, and a vantage point over the dining room with its red banquettes filled with fascinating parties. Spend at least part of an evening propped up at this bar, savoring the musty aura of an old New York where waiters wore uniforms and bow ties, and the fur and fedora-wearing clientele Brylcreemed their hair and smoked cigarettes from silver cases.

AVANT-GARDE PERFORMANCE SPACE
## 19 The Kitchen
512 West 19th Street

If a city is only as good as its experimental art, then this venue is a convincing argument for New York primacy. Founded in SoHo in 1971 by Woody and Steina Vasulka to present the then emerging genre of video art, The Kitchen

moved in the mid-1980s to a large building in Chelsea. With its gallery and large black-box theater, the space is like a general store for the avant garde. Presenting a wildly varied program of innovative artists on a weekly basis, a young team of curators draw from the fertile fields of dance, theater, performance art, literature and music. During the course of one week, The Kitchen has hosted an experimental pop violinist, a drag performance artist, and an open tap-dance jam.

IT ALL HAPPENED HERE
## 20 Hotel Chelsea
128

BASQUE ON THE WEST SIDE
## 21 Tía Pol
205 Tenth Avenue

Hitting all the hot spots of Chelsea can be a gruelling task: so many galleries, so little nourishment. But there's no better place to replenish than at Tía Pol, a bit of Basque on the West Side, where chef Andrew Donovan flies the flag for the small-plates trend that has overtaken Manhattan. Galleristas perch on stools in the narrow restaurant or crowd around tables at the back, munching on salt cod croquettes and periwinkles, Chinatown-style, all washed down with sangria, rioja and txakolina, an effervescent Basque wine.

UP ON THE ROOF
## 22 High Line Park
529 West 20th Street

As recently as the 1930s, New York was a train-and-boat trading city. To facilitate the flow of millions of tons of goods, the city spent $150 million building 13 miles (21 kilometers) of elevated track called the High Line. But by the 1950s highways had obviated its need and parts of the High Line were torn down. In 2001, conservationists appealed a demolition order by outgoing mayor Rudy Giuliani and began the process of converting the High Line into Manhattan's own Promenade Plantée. The ambitious design by Field Operations and Diller Scofidio + Renfro, consisting of tree-lined walks, amphitheaters and sundecks, playfully weaves in the old railroad tracks of the High Line's past life.

MEAT LOAF IN MARGARITAVILLE
## 23 The Rusty Knot
154

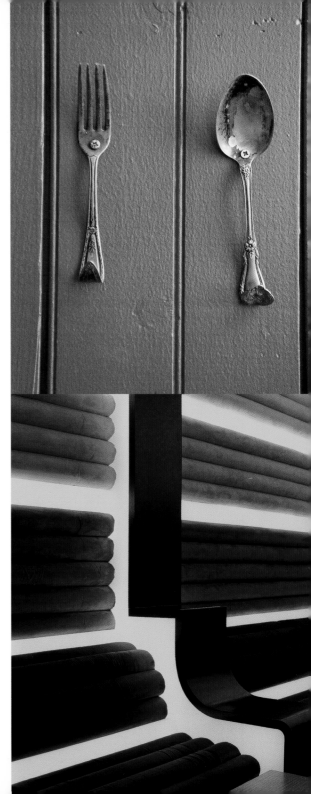

The Red Cat's menu reflects the warmth and comfort of the restaurant's ambience with unpretentious, well-executed American bistro dishes. If you do not feel like making the commitment to a shell steak with Yukon golds, fennel and aïoli with Cabernet sauce, then order some sides – particularly the parmesan French fries and red-hot rapini – to eat with a glass of excellent wine at the bar. The red and white barnwood interior has a New England feel, but the addition of huge hanging candle lanterns from Morocco saves it from cute pastiche.

La Lunchonette's friendly, slightly dishevelled interior is an inviting oasis and a welcome contrast to the desolate street it has inhabited since 1988. Chef Jean-François Fraysse and his wife, Melva Max, jointly own the place and serve up delicious French dishes such as lamb sausage with sautéed apples and pan-fried whole trout with wild mushrooms. On Sundays the restaurant features live jazz.

DJ Nicolas Matar runs a club with less attitude and more ambience than many of his competitors in the Meatpacking District. Inspired by the atmosphere of late 1980s New York nightlife, Matar focuses on the music above all else. As you'd expect of a former resident at Pacha in Ibiza, Matar's staple fare is house music, but at Cielo, it's eclectic, worldly and soulful enough to be interesting. Stephane Dupoux has surrounded the sunken dance floor with brown and beige suede banquettes, and enhanced the 1970s aesthetic with lighting effects.

PARISIAN BISTRO

**28 Pastis**

9 Ninth Avenue

Even though you know this is a pitch-perfect simulation, a Disneyfication of a Parisian bistro, there are moments (on a weekday morning, for example) when – with an espresso, a newspaper plucked from the rack just inside the door, and a sunlit breakfast spread out on your window-side table – it feels great. Restaurateur Keith McNally, whose other venues include Lucky Strike, Morandi, Schiller's Liquor Bar (p. 56) and Balthazar (p. 22), has surpassed himself with attention to detail in his conversion of a wholesale flower market into Pastis. Chefs Riad Nasr and Lee Hanson serve dishes inspired by hearty Provençal cuisine. Avoid the late-night invasion of uptowners and out-of-towners slumming it in the Meatpacking District, and limit yourself to daytime and early evening visits.

GASTROPUB IN THE CITY

**29 Spotted Pig**

314 West 11th Street

As New York's first – and only – gastropub, the Spotted Pig serves up the hearty fare of chef April Bloomfield, formerly of Chez Panisse and the River Café, as well as glimpses of A-listers on their way to the private third floor. Owner Ken Friedman describes the venue as a "country pub in the city with a bit of hunting-and-fishing lodge thrown in," and porcine paintings, bar stools and reclaimed wood floors continue the country theme. On the menu are classics like Devils on Horseback, along with house specialties such as sweet ricotta gnudi with brown butter and sage sauce. There's a Spotted Pig cask ale and a hog's heaven of beer on tap. Late night, the kitchen churns out crispy pig's ears, faggots and bath chaps to New Yorkers who pack in as tight as tinned sardines. But waiting for a table is all part of the experience. And you never know who you'll rub elbows with at the Spotted Pig.

CUPCAKE HEAVEN

**30 Magnolia Bakery**

401 Bleecker Street

The cupcakes under 1950s bell jars in the window of this chaotic, old-fashioned bakeshop, which has been serving sugar addicts since 1996, are what devotees travel from all over the world for. Pink, yellow and brown butter icing is slapped inches thick onto the palm-sized sponge cakes and then topped with lurid sprinkles. You can take the cupcakes away in boxes for parties, but most people choose to linger with their prize in the sugary steam of the café or on the small bench outside. And now uptowners have their very own slice of the Magnolia pie: a shop recently opened at 200 Columbus Avenue, on the corner of West 69th Street.

ALADDIN'S CAVE OF SHOES

**31 Jeffrey**

449 West 14th Street

When Jeffrey first opened on 14th Street in 1999, there were precious few other shops in the Meatpacking District. Taxicabs would eject fur-clad and Manolo-shod ladies who had to gingerly make their way past skinned carcasses swinging from the doorways of meat lockers to get to the mini-department store's front door. Today the contrasts are less stark and the gasps are reserved solely for the dazzling footwear displays – Jeffrey Kalinsky, the store's owner, was a former shoe buyer at Barneys (p. 162).

MOD COVETABLES

**32 Auto**

**33  Vitra Showroom**

29 Ninth Avenue

These offices and showroom for the Swiss furniture company Vitra were designed by architect-of-the-moment Lindy Roy. Her conversion of a turn-of-the-20th-century storage space is a study of sensual modernism. Three stories are connected by two slots that incorporate staircases, and large rubber-wrapped display surfaces that extend the floor area of the second-floor showroom down into the retail space and gallery below.

A FISHY TALE

**34  Mary's Fish Camp**

64 Charles Street

New York, strangely, does not want for fish shacks. There is the Pearl Oyster Bar, Jack's Oyster Bar, Ed's Fish Camp and Brooklyn Fish Camp, among others. They all are embroiled in some sort of acrimonious fish fight, but internecine struggle should be of little concern to diners. Instead, head directly to that embodiment of the New England fish shack aesthetic, Mary's Fish Camp, founded by Mary Redding in 2001. Inside the shanty-chic corner venue, tables are crowded close together and patrons share a hard wooden bench. A highlight of the menu is the lobster roll, an ungainly but delicious mound of fresh lobster meat and mayonnaise served on a warm hot dog bun next to a pile of shoestring fries. Not to be missed.

"WE LOVE MARC JACOBS"

**35  Marc Jacobs**

172

IT'S A WRAP

**36  Diane von Furstenberg**

874 Washington Street

For classically sexy wrap dresses in Von Furstenberg's signature prints and solid colors, head to her shimmering store in the far reaches of the West Village. The wraps, along with ruched tops, slim-fitting, ultra-suede trousers, and coordinating accessories, are presented in a space designed by BE Partners and Bill Katz. The wall and ceiling treatment consists of plaster spotted with flush, 4-inch (10-centimeter) mirror disks and halogen lamps. The dressing rooms, in the center of the store, are enclosed in a circle of ceiling-to-floor white silk draperies and the Furstenberg dotted logo is deployed on sandblasted glass pivot doors that separate the retail and event spaces.

TRAVEL KIT

**37  Flight 001**

96 Greenwich Avenue

Brad John and John Sencion have cornered the *Wallpaper\**-toting, wanderlust market with their mod West Village travel boutique. For real adventurers, there are travel guides, leather passport holders, backpacks, washbags and Braun travel clocks. And for the more armchair inclined, globes and coffee table books will fill many happy hours. Dario C. Antonio's design for the store includes rubber flooring, a glowing back wall, and universal travel symbols in powder blue for decorative detail.

BEER AND BURGERS

**38  Corner Bistro**

140

CULT DENIM

**39  Rag & Bone**

100 and 104 Christopher Street

Marcus Wainwright and David Neville, the two men behind new label Rag & Bone, have launched two large stores in which to showcase their refined but rugged designs. They opened, like the true Kentucky gentlemen they are, the women's and children's store first, but soon expanded to open the menswear store at 100 Christopher Street. Both stores are rough-hewn, just like the clothing. The womenswear designs would not be out of place in a Dorothea Lange photograph, albeit with a slightly sinister twist. And the menswear, which includes a line of boots and bespoke suits, boasts more than a hint of Amish chic.

GASLIT PHARMACY

**40  C.O. Bigelow Apothecaries**

414 Sixth Avenue

This 170-year-old apothecary is still outfitted with its original wood shelving, ceiling moldings and chandeliers. Delftware jars and historic prescriptions are interspersed with the merchandise on offer, which encompasses an in-house line of perfumed oils, Bigelow's own Alchemy range of makeup, and old American favorites like Calgon and Ivory. Illustrious former customers include Mark Twain, who lived around the corner at 21 Fifth Avenue.

MYTHICAL MERCHANDISE

**41  Castor & Pollux**

174

# Gramercy Park
# East Village
# Lower East Side
# Lower Manhattan

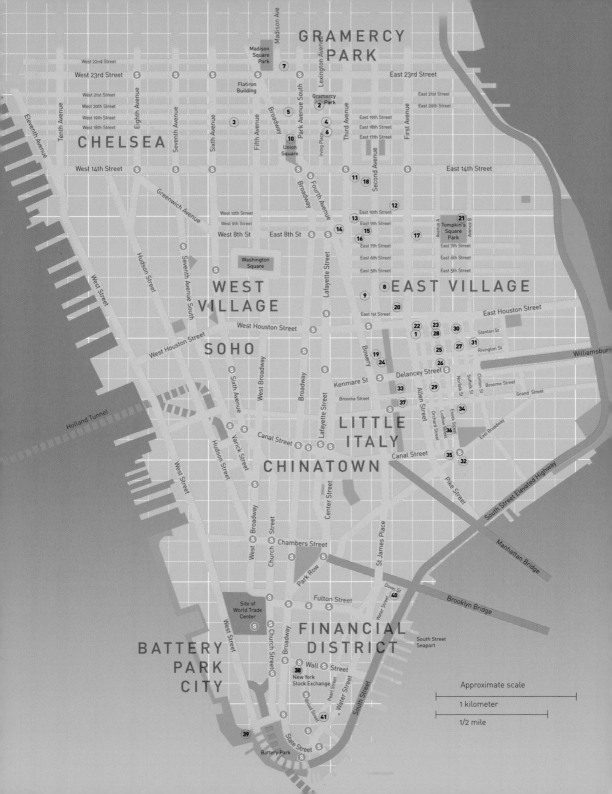

This exploration of the eastern flank of Manhattan begins at the island's well-fed right thigh and ends at its en pointe toe. In historical terms the journey runs counter to the city's evolution. Beginning with the once distant settlement of Gramercy Square, where the wealthiest knickerbockers congregated, it continues through the slums of the immigrant staging posts of the Lower East Side and finally arrives in the oldest part of New York, which was, from 1626 until becoming overcrowded in the mid-19th century, New York's chaotic center. Gramercy Park is the centerpiece of a historic district of tree-shaded streets lined with a variety of 19th-century residences, from 1840s row houses and brownstones to Victorian-era Queen Annes and neo-Gothics, which lend the area a particular gentility.

The East Village's history starts circa 1960, when it branched off from the Lower East Side as an area self-defined by its countercultural activity and centered around a few coffee houses and clubs near St. Mark's Place. The area was plagued with drug-related crime throughout the 1970s and 1980s, and provided the gritty backdrop for an exciting art and punk-rock scene. The Rudy Giuliani-administered clean-up of Tompkins Square Park (p. 56) in 1992 brought a trail of French bistros and media types in its wake, pushing the original residents and those who arrived too late to the southeast. These pioneers found themselves in a Lower East Side both stained and bespangled by its longstanding role as the immigrant gateway to the rest of New York. The first wave of arrivals took place in the 19th century, when political events in Europe and anti-Chinese sentiment on the West Coast fanned the sails of boatloads of settlers towards New York. In the 1960s, following a relaxation of immigration laws, streams of new colors, languages, religions and cultures formed vibrant and sometimes violent eddies in the area. The most recent flood of new blood is largely Puerto Rican, Dominican, and young white musicians and artists. Ludlow and Orchard Streets were the scenes of a severe attack of hipification in the 1990s, while Clinton and Rivington Streets are the ongoing sites of more recent and, thankfully, more considered creative intrusion.

Continuing south and further back in time you arrive at the narrow, tangled streets laid out by 17th-century Dutch settlers, when the city was still known as New Amsterdam. Among the closely packed top-heavy financial and Old World corporate centers, and smoky, back-alley taverns down crooked lanes that resisted the imposition of the 19th-century grid, it's easy to lose your sense of time and space — that is, until you emerge into the southernmost territory of the island, where a boat ride or walk across the Brooklyn Bridge (p. 60) provides an exhilarating view of the city.

EAST SIDE GLAMOUR

**1   Thompson Lower East Side**

GOTHIC ARCHITECTURE, MEMBERS ONLY

**2   National Arts Club**

15 Gramercy Park South

Built in 1845, this building has housed the National Arts Club and its members – the first of whom included Theodore Roosevelt and Woodrow Wilson – since 1906. Its original flat-front, iron-grilled appearance matched the style of the houses still maintained on the west side of Gramercy Park. But in the 1880s the mansion's owner, Samuel Tilden, hired Calvert Vaux – one of the designers of Central Park – to bring the façade up to tempo with the trend for High Victorian style. Vaux duly added bay windows, polychromatic brickwork and Gothic ornamentation. During exhibitions and events when the public is admitted, you can see the stained-glass ceilings that John LaFarge created for the inside of the building and the Italian carved fireplaces. You might even see Martin Scorsese, Ethan Hawke, Dennis Hopper and Uma Thurman, who are among the club's current members.

SALADS AND DOUBLE-CHOCOLATE COOKIES

**3   City Bakery**

3 West 18th Street

Visit City Bakery for a sublime chocolate experience that might include a "shot" of viscous dark chocolate scooped from a constantly churning vat, or a huge double-chocolate cookie freshly baked by pastry chef and owner, Maury Rubin. For lunch, this airy café, frequented by designers and photographers from the surrounding Flatiron district, has the best seasonal salad counter in town, assembled by chef Ilene Rosen. The bakery holds bizarre food festivals throughout the year, such as the "City Bakery State Fair" in July when the otherwise urbane space undergoes a country makeover with a carpet of hay, a picket fence and gingham-clad girls serving corn dogs and lemonade.

ALE AND WINGS SINCE 1864

**4   Pete's Tavern**

129 East 18th Street

The beating heart of Irving Place is an Irish saloon that has been serving "grocery and grog" since 1864. It even stayed open during Prohibition, disguised as a flower shop. Popular legend has it that one of the regulars, O. Henry, wrote his 1902 classic *Gift of the Magi* at the first booth by the door. Today the bar has an Italian-American menu, three television screens and a loyal crowd of after work drinkers. Pete's own 1864 Original Ale is still drawn from old porcelain taps set in the 30-foot-long (9-meter) rosewood bar.

A GOURMET COUNTRY REFUGE

**5   Gramercy Tavern**

42 East 20th Street

For some New American gastronomic indulgence, consider one of Tom Colicchio's tasting menus at the well-established and well-loved Gramercy Tavern, offering a sample of the restaurant's seasonal offerings and reaching a crescendo with Claudia Fleming's wonderful desserts, perhaps a mascarpone cream Napoleon with rhubarb compote and strawberries. For a less expensive alternative, there is the handsome bar in the festive Tavern Room at the front of the rustic-themed restaurant. With more than eighty-five selections, the cheese course ranks as one of the city's finest. Order a selection of three, six or ten as a dessert, or sample with wine at the bar. The service throughout is impeccable; service staff tell you how dishes taste, not just what's in them.

WHARTON-ESQUE RETREAT

**6   The Inn at Irving Place**

120

SPICE WORLD

**7   Tabla**

11 Madison Avenue

Young Bombay-born chef Floyd Cardoz fuses American and Indian cuisines at this flamboyantly designed restaurant in the Art Deco Metropolitan Life Tower. Dishes such as tandoori quail with black pepper glaze, taro-dusted halibut with white beans, and scallops in a mustard oil and red pepper coulis have earned Cardoz the adoring attention of New York food critics. The richly colored, curvy space features a suspended second floor around a "viewing well." Here you can snack on grape pine nut and tomato kalonji chutneys, or guacamole with toasted cumin on a variety of breads. The restaurant's owner is Danny Meyer, whose other smash successes are Union Square Café, Gramercy Tavern (see above) and Eleven Madison Park. For a taste of his style to go, try a gourmet-prepared hot dog from the shake shack located in the southeast corner of Madison Square Park.

ECCENTRIC VICTORIANA

BOHO-CHIC JEWELRY

IT'S EASY BEING GREEN
## 10 Greenmarket
Union Square, East 17th Street and Broadway

Before ducking underground to catch the L-train to Williamsburg (only two stops away), savor the smells and colors of the farmers' produce stalls that cluster at the northern end of Union Square. Dating from 1839, the square has been a traditional platform for political rallies and labor protests. The few remaining radicals now share the steps and railings with skateboarding tricksters and breakdancers, watched by yuppies having their lunch in the sunshine. The market is open Monday, Wednesday, Friday, and Saturday.

NO-FRILLS BEAUTY PRODUCTS

DELICIOUS DESSERT BAR
## 12 ChikaLicious
203 East 10th Street

This intimate, twenty-seat bôite is built around an open kitchen where chefs Don and Chika Tillman work and serve customers directly. There is a three-course prix-fixe menu for $12, including such "main courses" as honey parfait in blood orange soup with black tapioca and poppy seed lace crisp or a warm chocolate tart with pink peppercorn ice cream and red wine sauce. Recommended wines are listed with each choice on the menu.

BOOKMARK
## 13 St. Mark's Bookshop
31 Third Avenue

Established in 1977, St. Mark's is one of the last vestiges of the legendary East Village intellectual scene. Open until midnight every day of the week, the store is just as much a hangout spot for students and professionals as it is a repository of specialist books and periodicals. Categories include cultural theory, graphic design, poetry and film studies, as well as stock from small press publishers.

From the moment you descend the steps and ring the buzzer for this basement bar, you're submerged in a Japanese netherworld. Low lighting, an idiosyncratic soundtrack and kooky Japanese bar staff combine to create an atmosphere that can vary from subdued to wild in the space of one evening. The wooden bar in the front room conceals a den in the back for some seated sake and appetizer consumption. The okonomiyaki (Japanese pancake) is a house favorite.

When CBGB's closed and Whole Foods moved in, it seemed like the last shred of character of this historically seedy stretch of the Bowery had vanished. Fortunately, the new (it opened in 2007) New Museum, which rises into the air like an uneven stack of boxes, shows that quirkiness and character live on in this part of the city. Tokyo-based design studio SANAA covered the building in an aluminum grid, upon which Ugo Rondinone's rainbow sign "Hell, Yes!" aptly embodies the can-do zeitgeist. Exhibits range from an exploration of contemporary urban design ("Urban China: Informal Cities") to an installation of floating blue handballs called "Master Bait Me" by Agathe Snow.

INDIAN-INSPIRED THREADS

**20 Alpana Bawa**

70 East 1st Street

Punjab-born Alpana Bawa threads her Indian heritage into the fabric of her vivid and immaculately tailored clothing line. Her original construction methods and use of color have earned her "darling" status among fashion critics. Beaded evening gowns and pink and lilac tanks embroidered with leaves and vines are among the favorites of her female fans. Men, too, can strut their funky stuff in architecturally inspired shirts.

FROM LABOR PROTESTS TO LATTES

**21 Tompkins Square Park**

Avenues A to B, and East 7th to East 10th Streets

Though relatively small, Tompkins Square Park in the heart of the East Village has a big history behind it. Like Union Square a few blocks to the northwest (see Greenmarket; p. 54), Tompkins Square has traditionally been a meeting ground for protest gatherings. The most legendary of these, in 1988, devolved into the infamous Tompkins Square Park riots, sparked when police sought to evict drug dealers and the homeless from the park. But as the East Village as a whole became more gentrified, so, too, did the park. Today, the American elm-shaded paddocks and bench-lined paths are frequented by a mix of colorful local characters and latte-sipping yummy mummies and their offspring who gather for the weekly farmer's market.

CAVIAR AND PICKLES

**22 Russ & Daughters**

179 East Houston Street

Having opened his first store on Orchard Street in 1914, Joel Russ began serving schmaltz herring in a barrel and salt-cured lox at this location in the 1920s. His daughters – Hattie, Ida, and Anne – joined him at the spotless white-tiled counter in the 1940s. Now in its fourth generation of ownership, the delicatessen, which the Smithsonian Institution deems to be "part of New York's cultural heritage," is still going strong. People come from all over the city for gleaming beluga, osetra and sevruga caviar, smoked sturgeon, herring and salmon, as well as candied fruits and nuts. Just outside the door, you can check the time by the scrambled numbers on the clock on top of the Red Square apartment building, designed by Tibor Kalman.

I'LL HAVE WHAT SHE'S HAVING

**23 Katz's Delicatessen**

145

COMFORT FOOD

**24 Freeman's**

137

CANDIES GALORE

**25 Economy Candy**

108 Rivington Street

This cluttered candy warehouse has been selling jawbreakers, strawberry shoelaces and Atomic Fireballs for a penny a piece since 1937. The store's owner, Jerry Cohen, will climb a ladder to reach your favorite jar from the floor-to-ceiling shelves.

360-DEGREE DESIGN

**26 Hotel on Rivington**

132

BISTRO DINING

**27 Schiller's Liquor Bar**

131 Rivington Street

Some of the interior details at Schiller's, such as the white-tiled walls, hint at the site's previous incarnation as a pharmacy. As is often the case with New York's trendier restaurants, mornings and lunchtimes are best. Order a couple of freshly made dollar doughnuts to munch while you wait with your newspapers for a breakfast of eggs hussard, or sour cream and hazelnut waffles served with mixed berries and bourbon maple syrup.

## 28 TG170

170 Ludlow Street

Terry Gillis has launched many a fashion career from her pioneering store at 170 Ludlow. Her labels of choice include Pixie Yates, Living Doll, United Bamboo, Ulla Johnson and Liz Collins. Accessories include bags that range from the messenger functionality of Freitag, to the delicate whimsy of purses made from vintage kimono fabric. In the T-shirt department is Supersonic's hot dog-print muscle-tee, in addition to perennial favorites from Petit Bateau.

IMMIGRANT LIFE

## 29 Lower East Side Tenement Museum

97 Orchard Street

Made up of a series of tenement buildings and accessible by guided tour only, this fascinating museum explores the experiences of immigrants in the late 19th century. The Lower East Side is referred to as the "gateway to America" for the vast number of immigrants it has housed (often in appalling conditions) over the years. The tenement at 90 Orchard Street, for example, was home to an estimated 7,000 people from more than twenty nations between 1863 and 1935. It has now been restored to allow a glimpse into the lives of residents from different historical periods.

ROMANTIC GERMAN SYNAGOGUE

## 30 Angel Orensanz Foundation

172 Norfolk Street

This synagogue was commissioned from architect Alexander Seltzer in 1849 by members of the German Jewish community, who arrived in Manhattan in the 1840s. In 1986, the sculptor Angel Orensanz bought the decaying building and saved it from demolition. Now the neo-Gothic space, with its 50-foot-high (15-meter) ceilings, is rented out for candlelit parties and cultural events such as Alexander McQueen's first American show and Rainer Werner Fassbinder's *Garbage, the City and Death*.

GOURMAND'S STRIP

## 31 Clinton Street

- Frankie's Spuntino, no. 17
- WD–50, no. 50
- Alias Café, no. 76

Under the shadow of the Williamsburg Bridge, Clinton Street has become the Lower East Side's "Restaurant Row." In the space of a couple of blocks are WD-50, Wylie

Dufresne's world-famous mecca of molecular gastronomy (try the everything bagel and smoked salmon "threads"); Alias Café, serving informal yet contemporary riffs on comfort food such as a fresh strawberry, fried caper and ricotta salad; and, at no. 17, Frankie's Spuntino, the cozy Manhattan outpost of restaurateurs Frank Falcinelli and Frank Castronovo. From within the Edison lightbulb-lit, exposed brick parlor of a restaurant, the Franks, as they're known, serve an impressive variety of homemade Italian dishes, including cavatelli served with pork sausage from Faicco's Pork Store (260 Bleecker Street), an old-school Italian butcher.

A BEAST OF A BAR

## 32 B.East

150

CHINA ON THE CHEAP

## 33 Dumpling House

118 Eldridge Street

If you long for the alleys of Beijing, visit this hole-in-the-wall dumpling house where the food – and the prices – are absolutely authentic. Feast on five pork-and-chive dumplings for one dollar, and add a sesame pancake to mop up the hot sauce for another fifty cents. Once a closely guarded secret, the word is now out. While you wait in line for your Styrofoam take-out container, owner Vanessa Duan and staff prepare your food over steaming pans and spitting skillets.

DOUGHNUTS, DAHLING!

## 34 Doughnut Plant

379 Grand Street

From the street you can observe the inner workings of this Roald Dahl-esque factory as it produces an eye-popping selection of enormous handglazed doughnuts. The colorful confections are baked to an old Lower East Side family recipe that has been passed down to current proprietor, Mark Isreal. The list of choices is long and always changing, to include seasonally inspired varieties like pumpkin, nostalgic ones like malted milk, and the perennially delicious Valrhona-Chocolate.

CREATIVE ENDEAVOR

## 35 Project No. 8

165

## 36 Brown Café + Orange
61 Hester Street

Mexican-born surfer/chef Alejandro Alcocer converted this tiny gallery space into a café ostensibly to provide good coffee to an espresso-deprived neighborhood. He also brought in good simple foods, such as French cheese and raisin walnut bread, sourced during a decade of global travel prior to settling in the Lower East Side. These items are sold at Orange, the delicatessen half of the enterprise. Regular brunchers at Brown Café recommend the Tuscan breakfast platter. Green is the catering arm of the venture.

REGGAE RAPTURE
## 37 Deadly Dragon Sound System
102b Forsyth Street

After three years of causing a ruckus in Chicago's reggae community, in 1998 Deadly Dragon Sound System moved to New York. With more than 150,000 pieces of vinyl and acetate in its vaults, ranging from classic Ska numbers to more contemporary interpretations, this store is a prized resource for reggae browsers and fanatics alike.

TEMPLE TO MONEY
## 38 New York Stock Exchange
8 Broad Street

Built in 1903 by George B. Post, this marble money temple's two-story base and Corinthian columns signify permanence and power. Although visitors are currently not able to view the frenetic trading floor, the Exchange is an appropriate starting point for an exploration into the district's fusion of finance and power architecture. The Museum of American Financial History (24 Broadway) tells the history of Wall Street through displays of ancient ticker-tape machines, telegraphs and trading tables. If you book well ahead, you can also visit the Federal Reserve Bank of New York (33 Liberty Street), which holds the nation's largest store of gold. The limestone-clad skyscraper of the Bank of New York (1 Wall Street and Broadway) was built in 1932 and its banking hall is an Art Deco feast of gold, orange, and red mosaic tiles.

HIGH-RISE HISTORIES
## 39 Skyscraper Museum
39 Battery Place

At the base of the Ritz Carlton Hotel in Battery Park, the long-migratory Skyscraper Museum has finally found a permanent home. Designed by skyscraper titans Skidmore, Owings & Merrill, the facility contains one gallery devoted to the evolution of New York's commercial skyline, and another to changing shows that explore aspects of high-rise building. An after-museum cocktail in the hotel's 14th-floor Rise bar affords clear views across the harbor to the Statue of Liberty. Alternatively, a sea-breezy walk across Battery Park takes you to the Staten Island Ferry terminal. From here you can ride to and from Staten Island (about thirty minutes each way), taking in close-up views of Alexandre Gustave Eiffel's Statue of Liberty on the way out, and on the return, a southerly perspective of the high-rises of Lower Manhattan, all for no charge.

ROMANCING THE BRIDGE
## 40 Bridge Café
279 Water Street

A decorative pressed-tin ceiling, ample windows displaying the Manhattan-bound arches of the Brooklyn Bridge, and a setting in one of the city's oldest food-service buildings are just a few features that make the delightfully snug and (in the evening) positively romantic Bridge Café worth a visit. Once sated, walk the pedestrian platform that traverses the outer edge of Brooklyn Bridge, that lyrical 1883 construction of soaring steel-wire cables and neo-Gothic towers that was at one time the largest suspension bridge in the world and the first to be constructed in steel. On the far side is Brooklyn Heights, a small enclave of early and mid-19th-century brownstones and brick houses, once the homes of prosperous ship captains and now populated by wealthy filmmakers and stockbrokers. Stroll the Brooklyn Heights Promenade between Cranberry and Remsen Streets for a view of Lower Manhattan's skyline, especially magical at sunset.

A COLONIAL INN
## 41 Fraunces Tavern
54 Pearl Street

In the final days of the Revolutionary War, the Fraunces Tavern served as George Washington's residence, and it was in the Long Room that he delivered his farewell to the officers of the Continental Army on December 4, 1783 before returning to his residence at Mount Vernon. In 1904 the historic significance of the then decaying building was realized, and it was reconstructed to look like a late 18th-century inn. Today, it is Wall Street traders that frequent the colonial-style street-level dining room. On the upper floors is a museum, which, if a little dusty, has a certain charm.

# Midtown

Approximate scale

1/2 kilometer

1/4 mile

**Central Park**

Central Park Zoo

The Pond

Central Park South

**LENOX HILL**

East 73rd Street
East 72nd Street
East 70th Street
East 70th Street
East 69th Street
Ⓢ East 68th Street
East 67th Street
East 66th Street
East 65th Street
East 64th Street
Ⓢ East 63rd Street
East 62nd Street
East 61st Street
East 60th Street

Queensboro

Madison Avenue
Park Avenue
Lexington Avenue
Third Avenue
Second Avenue
First Avenue
York Avenue

Franklin D. Roosevelt Drive

Fifth Avenue

Ⓢ
㉖ Columbus Circle

West 58th Street
㉙ West 57th Street Ⓢ
West 56th Street
West 55th Street
West 54th Street
㉘
West 53rd Street
**MIDTOWN**
West 52nd Street
West 51st Street
㉓
Radio City Music Hall
West 50th Street
West 49th Street
Rockefeller Center
Rockefeller Plaza
West 48th Street
West 47th Street
㉛
West 46th Street
Broadway
West 45th Street
West 44th Street
㉑ ㉚
West 43rd Street
㉕ Times Square
West 42nd Street Ⓢ Ⓢ
Port Authority Bus Terminal
West 41st Street
Bryant Park
New York Public Library ⑦
㉗
West 40th Street
West 39th Street
West 38th Street
West 37th Street
West 36th Street

Eighth Avenue
Broadway
Seventh Avenue
Sixth Avenue

**GARMENT DISTRICT**

⑱

Ⓢ East 59th Street
⑰ ⑯
East 58th Street
East 57th Street
⑲
⑫
⑬
⑳
East 56th Street
East 55th Street
⑳
㉒
East 54th St
East 53rd Street Ⓢ
③
⑪
⑮ ⑩ Seagram Building
East 52nd Street
East 51st Street
**TURTLE BAY**
East 50th St
East 49th St
East 48th St
East 47th St
East 46th St
East 45th St
East 44th St
Vanderbilt Avenue
Grand Central Station ②
Depew Place
East 43rd St ⑧ Chrysler Building
East 42nd Street
East 41st Street
East 40th Street
East 39th Street
East 38th Street
East 37th Street
East 36th Street

Ⓢ East 59th Street
Queensboro

⑨ United Nations Headquarters

Sutton Place

Second Avenue
Third Avenue
First Avenue

Queens - Midtown Tu

Franklin D. Roosevelt Drive

Pierpont Morgan Library ①

**MURRAY HILL**

㉔ ⑤

Midtown is New York at its most vertiginous and luminous. On street level, the traffic lights turn and the crowds cross the grids like clockwork. Overhead, the lofty ambitions of mid-century modernist architecture reach toward infinity. From broad-shouldered corporate headquarters along the "Park Avenue Corridor" to the designer flagships of Fifth Avenue, from the fiberoptic stars that twinkle on the ceiling of Grand Central Station (p. 66) to the cacophony of Times Square (p. 74), Midtown condenses and amplifies the energy of the city in ways that are both exhausting and exhilarating. Among the pillars of commerce are some pioneers of 1950s "glass box" architecture, including Mies van der Rohe's Seagram Building (see Brasserie, p. 71, and the Four Seasons Bar, p. 159), and the newly restored Lever House by Skidmore, Owings & Merrill (see Lever House Restaurant, p. 143), the city's first building to be constructed entirely from steel and glass. The postmodern response came in the improbable forms of Philip Johnson's Lipstick Building and Chippendale breakfront top for AT&T (now owned by Sony), along with Edward Barnes's black granite prism for IBM.

Grand Central Station, designed in 1913 and newly emerged from a decade-long renovation program, combines an extraordinary feat of urban planning — multilevel circulation for cars, trains, subways and pedestrians — and magnificent Beaux Arts architecture. The terminal was preserved after many years of decline, thanks to a campaign spearheaded by Jacqueline Onassis. Penn Station, southwest of Grand Central at 8th Avenue and 31st Street, was not so lucky. The 1910 building designed by McKim, Mead & White, a noble gateway to the city, was unceremoniously torn down in the 1960s and replaced by a nondescript cat-flap of an entryway. Now, the General Post Office across the street is being transformed by SOM into a new station with a soaring arch of steel and glass.

In the latter half of the 19th century, Midtown was the city's most fashionable residential neighborhood. The Vanderbilts alone had four mansions between 34th and 59th Streets. Today, little remains of this genteel past except for the two exquisite buildings that now house Cartier (653 Fifth Avenue) and Versace (675 Fifth Avenue). The new occupants of Fifth Avenue are flagship shops — Tiffany's (p. 71), Calvin Klein, Gucci — and upmarket department stores — Henri Bendel, Bergdorf Goodman, Barneys (p. 162) — that emit their distilled essences via the streams of shopping bags that flow up and down the thoroughfare. Midtown is also the center of the city's media and publishing industries. At the power-lunch hour, when television, magazine and web executives sally forth to Michael's or the Four Seasons, the river of shopping totes absorbs tributaries of briefcases and laptop cases from which protrude furled copies of the *New York Times*, the *New Yorker* or *Harper's*.

THE GILDED AGE

**1** **Morgan Library**

225 Madison Avenue

By 1906, J. Pierpont Morgan, banker, philanthropist and collector, needed a building in which to house his amazing collection of rare books, Old Master drawings and autographed manuscripts. Charles McKim gave him an Italian Renaissance-style palazzo with three magnificent rooms epitomizing America's Age of Elegance. Among the highlights of the library, located in Murray Hill, are three copies of the Gutenberg Bible, Charles Dickens's manuscript of *A Christmas Carol*, Henry David Thoreau's journals and Thomas Jefferson's letters to his daughter, Martha. There is a pleasant courtyard café, but if you're in the mood for something stronger, duck down into the dark hideaway of the Andrée Putman-designed Morgans Bar, beneath Morgans Hotel (237 Madison Avenue at 37th Street).

MONUMENT TO MOVEMENT

**2** **Grand Central Station + Campbell Apartment**

87 East 42nd Street

There's plenty to do at this 1913 Beaux Arts terminal without ever stepping foot on a train, from observing the 300,000 commuters deftly avoiding obstacles en masse like schools of fish to watching the light flood through the magnificent clerestory windows. Floating above the hustle and bustle, the Campbell Apartment is a gilded respite for the weary traveler. The bar, housed in the former office of 1920s businessman John Campbell, did time as a jail before it was renovated in 1999. Today it boasts golden murals, lush ruby banquettes, an intricately painted wood-beam ceiling and first-rate cocktails. It's something of a time warp, too. Concessions to the modern era of informality like athletic shoes, baseball caps and sweatshirts are prohibited.

**3  Paley Park**

East 53rd Street, between Madison and Fifth Avenues

An oasis in a concrete jungle, this delightful tiny park dating from 1967 uses its intensely urban setting to its advantage. A massive waterfall obliterates the sound of traffic, and seventeen honey locust trees provide welcome shade for a peaceful lunch. The park was funded by William Paley, former chairman of CBS, who was involved in every aspect of the design, right down to the selection of the hot dog stand. Paley Park was a favorite spot of urban theorist William "Holly" Whyte, who, when the park first opened, used time-lapse photography to show how people used public urban spaces.

OYSTER VAULT

**4  Grand Central Oyster Bar & Restaurant**

141

ALL THE ART YOU CAN EAT

**5  Museum of Modern Art +**
**Bar Room at the Modern**

11 and 9 West 53rd Street

Next door to the ever-resurgent Museum of Modern Art, which is settling comfortably into its new Yoshio Taniguchi-designed home, the Bar Room at the Modern offers refined and sophisticated food and drinks to soothe the soul after a day spent at this mammoth temple to contemporary art. With views over the Sculpture Garden and a seasonal outdoor terrace, this least formal of the museum's restaurants features the French-American cuisine of chef Gabriel Kreuther. Danish furniture and tableware, along with a huge forest image on the wall by German artist Thomas Demand, add detail to the open Bentel & Bentel-designed space.

BIBLIOPHILES' PARADISE
## 7 New York Public Library
Fifth Avenue at 42nd Street

Completed in 1911, the Carrère and Hastings-designed library, built to house the collection of the wealthy bibliophile John Astor, is a masterpiece of Beaux Arts design. If you take a tour, a docent will lead you around a dozen or so of the rooms, including one containing Charles Dickens's writing desk. Alternatively you can wander at your leisure through the rows of researchers in the finely restored Rose Main Reading Room or stand in the Astor Hall lobby, seemingly carved from one giant piece of marble, and contemplate the inherent contradictions of an institution built for public access yet financed by the robber barons of the late 19th century. The library also puts on many excellent exhibitions, and lunch can be had within paces of its magnificent steps. The Bryant Park Grill is right behind the library in a park that shows outdoor movie classics in the summer, and Ilo is a gourmet restaurant in the Bryant Park Hotel on East 40th Street.

ART DECO SKYSCRAPER
## 8 Chrysler Building
405 Lexington Avenue

New York's best-loved and most glorious skyscraper is an Art Deco classic. Even if you've seen it a thousand times before, there are moments when it can still take your breath away. When a glancing sunbeam lifts your gaze to its Nirosta stainless-steel crown – modeled after a Chrysler radiator grille – or at dusk, when its triangular-shaped windows set in layered scallops begin to emit their white light, William Van Alen's optimistic vision of the future holds true. You see the 1930 building in your mind's eye, like all of New York, from afar. An up-close visit, however, with your head tilted back, rewards you with a different perspective. Automobile-themed, handcrafted ornaments such as brickwork cars are at the base of the tower, and eagles in place of gargoyles lean out at the building's 61st floor. The lofty crown jewel of the building – the Cloud Room, a 1930s speakeasy with pink marble bathrooms and a gleaming bar of Bavarian wood – is out of bounds, unless you have the gall of tour operator Timothy "Speed" Levitch in the documentary, *The Cruise*. Until it is restored you will have to content yourself with the lobby, lined with red African marble, the murals and the marquetry on the elevator doors.

INTERNATIONAL TERRITORY
## 9 United Nations Headquarters
First Avenue at 46th Street

In 1947 an international group of architects convened in New York under the supervision of Wallace K. Harrison. Their mission was to produce a home for the newly formed United Nations, but, thanks to Le Corbusier's loudly voiced vision, the end result was much more than that. The United Nations complex is nothing short of an architectural icon signaling both modernity and world peace. The optimism of the project was reflected in Hitchcock's lens as he lingeringly drew down the green-tinted glass façade of the Secretariat Building in the opening scene of his 1959 movie, *North by Northwest*. Today the interior has a faded quality captured most poignantly by Adam Bartos's photographs in the book *International Territory: The UN 1945–1995*. You can dine with diplomats in the Delegates Dining Room, the windows of which give capacious views across the East River. The term 'international cuisine' is taken very literally at this lunch buffet, and every month features a different country's national repertoire.

POWER DRINKING
**10 Four Seasons Bar**

159

ENTIRELY SUITABLE
## 11 Steven Salen Tailors
18 East 53rd Street

A suite of wood-paneled rooms is the genteel site for this old-fashioned, no-nonsense tailors' business. The establishment was once patronized by Ernest Hemingway, upon the recommendation of his friend Gerald Murphy – the dapper artist upon whom F. Scott Fitzgerald based the character Dick Driver in *Tender is the Night*. Murphy advised Hemingway that Steven Salen was a "very good reliable old New York house, no chi-chi." Whether you want an entire wardrobe custom-made for summering on the Riviera or a minor alteration, you can trust a tailor that in 1933 placed an advertisement in *Fortune* magazine reading, "As formal clothes are conspicuous whatever the occasion, it is essential that such clothes be cut only by those who understand the basic laws of dress, otherwise the individual is in grave danger of paying a goodly sum for an entirely unsuitable outfit."

BLUE BOXES OF DELIGHT

### 12  Tiffany's
Fifth Avenue at 57th Street

You can't approach the door of Tiffany's without picturing Holly Golightly in Givenchy, dark glasses and pearls, sipping coffee and gazing wistfully at the treasures displayed in the window. If, like Holly in *Breakfast at Tiffany's*, your "reds" can be soothed away by a small pale-blue box, then head for this emporium of expensive jewels. Established in 1837, the store enjoyed its heyday at the turn of the 20th century, when Louis Comfort Tiffany, son of the store's founder, began designing his famous lamps and decadent Art Nouveau jewelry and enamels. Today the store's star designers are Elsa Peretti and Paloma Picasso.

MIDTOWN MERRIMENT

### 13  King Cole Bar

NEW STANDARDS

### 14  Brasserie
Seagram Building, 100 East 53rd Street

When the original Brasserie, located in the basement of Mies van der Rohe's Seagram Building, was destroyed by fire, architects Diller + Scofidio redesigned the restaurant with a nod to its heritage. As patrons had to descend perilously steep steps in the past, a new central glass staircase was introduced, pitched at a shallow angle. Interior details include flatscreen video monitors above the bar that capture diners' abrupt entry from the reception area, tables that are slabs of translucent lime-cast resin, and white leather "Executives" chairs by Eero Saarinen. Chef Luc Dimnet has created a contemporary menu with Brasserie classics indicated in bold face. For dessert, the chocolate beignets are perfect for sharing.

MODERNIST SANCTUARY

### 15  Lever House Restaurant
143

LAST OF THE GREATS

### 16  Le Cirque
142

CLEAN LINES

### 17  Linda Dresner
484 Park Avenue

Since 1985 Linda Dresner has offered clean-lined haute couture at her Park Avenue boutique, and is credited with being the first to bring Jil Sander's minimalist garments to New York. Using light as an integral component of the architecture, designer Michael Gabellini employed natural materials such as limestone, marble, granite, black macassar ebony, and nickel silver to create an eminently luxurious environment for equally high-caliber couture.

OLD NEWS, NEW BUILDING

### 18  New York Times Building
620 Eighth Avenue

In 1904, the *New York Times* moved to Longacre Square, an intersection soon redubbed Times Square (see p. 74). But in 2007, the newspaper moved west to brand-new premises designed by architect Renzo Piano. His 52-foot-high (16-meter) tower is a study in light and lines, enshrouded in a "sun screen" of ceramic tubes that take on the color of the sky. Public interest in the building has been intense. In 2008, two men were arrested for scaling the sides of the tower.

TRUNK SHOW

### 19  Louis Vuitton
1 East 57th Street

Peter Marino designed the interior of this newly opened 20,000-square-foot (1,860-square-meter) retail cathedral, in which vintage trunks and red hatboxes hang from the ceiling. The interior fittings and furnishings knowingly play upon the Louis Vuitton checkerboard theme, and the largest square is a three-story high LED screen that is visible from the street.

ANTICIPATING THE GUGGENHEIM

### 20  Mercedes-Benz Showroom
430 Park Avenue

This tiny showroom designed by Frank Lloyd Wright in 1954 can hold only five cars, positioned around a circular, sloping ramp – a mini forerunner of the rotunda at the Guggenheim Museum, some thirty blocks uptown. The geometry of the large circular mirror in the ceiling exploits the three-pointed star of Mercedes-Benz.

**21 Algonquin Hotel**

59 West 44th Street

The hotel lobby is the site of the historic Round Table at which, during the heady 1920s, Dorothy Parker pitted her acerbic wit against fellow literati. The Oak Room puts on cabaret acts every night of the week (except Monday), but it is the smaller round tables of the utterly unfashionable and slightly dusty Blue Bar that you should head for. Its walls are decorated with the artwork of long-time Algonquin regular Al Hirschfeld, and its uniformed waiters, with their inscrutable demeanors, serve pub fare and well-made Martinis. Just remember Parker's wisdom on that subject: "I like to have a Martini/Two at the very most/After three I'm under the table/After four I'm under the host."

JAPANESE DEPARTMENT STORE

**22 Takashimaya**

693 Fifth Avenue

From lacquered soup bowls to green seaweed flakes to monochromatic flower arrangements, this Japanese department store provides seven floors of accoutrements for recreating a perfectly imperfect wabi-sabi lifestyle. The initial design for the store followed Japanese tradition, which designates the first two floors as gallery space. The 1997 renovation, however, called for 3,000 square feet (279 square meters) of this space to be given over to luggage and travel accessories. Design firm S. Russell Groves solved the problem by creating an open grid system of ebonized ash shelves and low tables on which to display the larger luggage, and vitrines lined with Hunan silk for smaller articles. The top floor is devoted to high-end hair and beauty products, and the basement reveals the restful Tea Box café, where you are reminded why it is you are here and not at Macy's.

SOCIAL CLUB

**23 Russian Samovar**

256 West 52nd Street

Join Russian intellectuals, writers, artists and sometimes Mikhail Baryshnikov (who is part-owner and frequent patron) at the long smoky bar for a warming shot of horseradish vodka. Rousing traditional Russian folk tunes that are often sung around the piano may persuade you to stay. Pick from a rainbow of vodkas flavored in-house or from a menu strong on blinis and caviar, borscht, satsivi chicken, beef stroganoff, and smoked fish. If you don't have the time to visit the rowdy Russian enclave in Brooklyn's Brighton Beach, the Russian Samovar is a fine alternative. Many of the diners and drinkers engage in gesticulatory repartee with the owner, Roman Kaplan. One former regular was the poet Joseph Brodsky, and poetry readings held in his honor regularly take place at the restaurant.

SPATIAL CRAFTS

**24 American Folk Art Museum**

45 West 53rd Street

Tod Williams and Billie Tsien's beautifully considered new home for the American Folk Art Museum threw down the gauntlet for Yoshio Taniguchi's expanded Museum of Modern Art (p. 67) on the same block. The architects' solution for the interior combines monumentality and intimacy in perfect proportion. The museum has opened to much critical acclaim: architectural commentator Paul Goldberger has likened it to Sir John Soane's Museum in London for its "truly original spatial exercises within the townhouse volume." The museum's exhibitions live up to their surroundings – a recent breakthrough show was a retrospective of self-taught outsider artist, Henry Darger. The range of decorative, functional and ceremonial folk art to be found on display includes pottery, trade signs, quilts, and wind-up toys.

### BRIGHT LIGHTS, BIGGER SIGNS
## 25 Times Square
Broadway and Seventh Avenue,
between West 42nd and West 47th Streets

New York's most famous square is in fact an elongated intersection where Broadway crosses Fifth Avenue, and was named after the office block which housed the *New York Times* in the early 1900s (the newspaper has since moved on to pastures new at Eighth Avenue; see p. 71). The building was the world's first in 1928 to display a zipper sign, on which the newspaper posted election returns. Ever since, buildings around the square have competed for ownership of the biggest and brightest signs. Little Lulu and her Kleenex box, the puffing Camel smoker, and the various neon displays that once wowed the passing public now seem quaint exercises in restraint given the recent profusion of kinetic video monitors and jumbo digital displays that have enough candlepower to be visible at noon. Also of note in the square is the US Armed Forces Recruiting Station, designed by Architecture Research Office.

### LOLLIPOP BUILDING REBORN
## 26 Museum of Arts and Design
2 Columbus Circle

In 2008, the strange white marble building on Columbus Circle, dating from 1964 and which had stood vacant for years, was reborn as the Museum of Arts and Design. While keeping the general form of Edward Durrell Stone's Lollipop Building, so-called for the still extant "lollipop" columns, architecture firm Allied Design replaced the marble façade with some 20,000 handcrafted terracotta tiles, cut a squiggle of breaks in the front to allow light to stream in, and opened up the galleries from cramped quarters to flowing space. The current tenant fills the space with the wide-ranging objects from its collection, including Wharton Esherick's hammer-handle chairs and the early modernist jewelry of Margaret De Patta, among hundreds of other pieces.

### PAPER ART
## 27 Kinokuniya
1073 Avenue of the Americas

This Manhattan branch of global brand Kinokuniya is a bit of a mess, but that just makes locating your manga, graphic novels, origami paper, and exquisite Japanese stationery and notebooks all the more rewarding.

### SENSURROUND CINEMA
## 28 Ziegfeld Theater
141 West 54th Street

This fabulous movie theater sits on the site of the original "Ziegfeld Follies." Its massive screen, elegant red decor and impeccable sound and projection quality make it the perfect venue for the kinds of big action epics where you want to share your gasps and tears with 1,200 other moviegoers.

### PIANO FORTE
## 29 Steinway & Sons
109 West 57th Street

Steinway & Sons was founded in 1853 by German immigrant Henry Engelhard Steinway in a loft on Varick Street. The first piano produced by the company, number 483, was sold to a New York family for $500 and is now displayed in the Metropolitan Museum of Art (p. 82). In response to huge demand – thanks to the piano's role as the Victorian answer to a television – the Steinway business grew to include a factory town in Astoria, Queens, and a 2,000-seat concert hall on 14th Street. The remaining bastion of the piano-maker's empire is this neoclassical showroom on 57th Street designed in the mid-1920s by Grand Central Station's architects, Whitney Warren and Charles Wetmore. Behind the two-story rotunda you will find a stunning display, several soundproofed rooms deep, of every kind of grand, baby grand and upright instrument in every finish imaginable.

### QUIETLY ECLECTIC
## 30 City Club Hotel

118

### PORTABLE GLASS AND STEEL
## 31 Mies Design Shop
319 West 47th Street

Chris Masaoay, former buyer for the Cooper-Hewitt's museum shop (for the museum itself, see p. 82), stocks this Hell's Kitchen design outpost with housewares, gadgets and collectibles that reflect the aesthetic spirit of its modernist namesake.

# Upper East Side
# Upper West Side
# Harlem

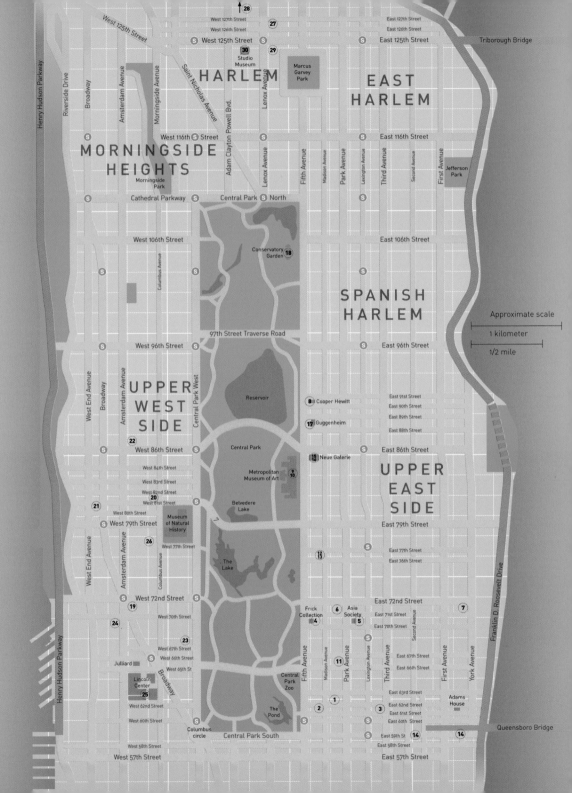

West 127th Street
28
27
West 126th Street
East 127th Street
East 126th Street
West 125th Street
West 125th Street
30
29
East 125th Street
Triborough Bridge

HARLEM
EAST
HARLEM

Studio Museum

Marcus Garvey Park

West 116th Street
116th Street
East 116th Street

MORNINGSIDE
HEIGHTS

Morningside Park

Jefferson Park

Cathedral Parkway
Central Park North

West 106th Street
East 106th Street

Conservatory Garden
18

SPANISH
HARLEM

97th Street Traverse Road

West 96th Street
East 96th Street

Reservoir

UPPER
WEST
SIDE

Cooper Hewitt
8
East 91st Street
East 90th Street

Guggenheim
17
East 89th Street
East 88th Street

West 86th Street
22
West 86th Street
East 86th Street

West 84th Street
Neue Galerie
15
16

West 83rd Street
Central Park

UPPER
EAST
SIDE

West 82nd Street
20
Metropolitan Museum of Art
9
10

West 81st Street

West 80th Street
21
Belvedere Lake

West 79th Street
West 79th Street
East 79th Street

Museum of Natural History
26
West 77th Street

12
13
East 77th Street
East 76th Street

The Lake

West 72nd Street
East 72nd Street

19
West 70th Street
Frick Collection
6
Asia Society
7

24
Julliard
23
West 67th Street
4
5
East 71st Street
East 70th Street

Lincoln Center
West 66th Street
West 65th St
11
East 67th Street
East 66th Street

25
West 62nd Street
Central Park Zoo
East 63rd Street

West 60th Street
Adams House

Columbus circle
2
1
3
East 62nd Street
East 61st Street
East 60th Street

The Pond
14
14

Central Park South
East 59th St
Queensboro Bridge

West 57th Street
East 58th Street
East 57th Street

Henry Hudson Parkway
Riverside Drive
Broadway
Amsterdam Avenue
Morningside Avenue
Saint Nicholas Avenue
Adam Clayton Powell Blvd.
Lenox Avenue
Fifth Avenue
Madison Avenue
Park Avenue
Lexington Avenue
Third Avenue
Second Avenue
First Avenue
West End Avenue
Central Park West
Columbus Avenue
York Avenue
Franklin D. Roosevelt Drive

Approximate scale
1 kilometer
1/2 mile

The Upper East Side is one of the city's most enduring prestigious neighborhoods. Its zip code, 10021, is the wealthiest in the nation and explains the concentration of classy boutiques and European patisseries on Madison Avenue. The original owners of the Fifth and Park Avenue mansions, families such as the Whitneys, the Astors, the Straights, the Dillons, the Dukes, the Mellons and the Pulitzers, all moved here from downtown in the late 1800s with the opening of Central Park. Today many of these grand homes house the city's most venerable museums.

The Upper West Side has its own museums, including the American Museum of Natural History with its newly added Rose Center for Earth and Space, an enormous white sphere suspended in a glass and wire cube. Its residents are stereotypically thought of as intellectually and politically liberal. The Upper West Side is also known for its grand apartment buildings, such as the San Remo, with its ornate twin towers concealing water tanks, and the Dakota on the edge of the park at 72nd Street, which is, at 125 years old, a grandfather of a New York luxury apartment. The Dakota (named as a joke at the time of its building in 1884 for its "far western" location) is a sought-after address, despite its notoriety as the location for the disturbing movie *Rosemary's Baby* and the place where resident John Lennon was shot. Strawberry Fields, Yoko Ono's memorial to the Beatle, landscaped by Bruce Kelly in 1983, is just a little way into the park outside the Dakota.

The area of Manhattan north of Central Park was covered with wooded hills and valleys and inhabited by Indians when the Dutch started the settlement of Nieuw Haarlem in 1658. A late-19th-century building boom, stimulated by the extension of subways to the north of the island, went bust and African-Americans who had been pushed out of other areas began to rent the empty apartment buildings. By the 1910s Harlem had become the biggest black community in the United States, and all through the 1920s and 1930s blacks streamed in from the southern states to feed a cultural explosion known as the Harlem Renaissance. The Sugar Cane Club and the Cotton Club hosted Count Basie, Duke Ellington, and countless others. Lena Horne got her start here, and literary giants Langston Hughes and James Baldwin were native sons. Today, although Harlem's historic liberators and orators are written into its streets and institutions, and even though a handful of jazz clubs still survive, the neighborhood is mostly forward-looking. Violent crime, which had plagued its streets, has been significantly reduced and in 2001 former President Bill Clinton moved his office to 55 West 125th Street, just two factors in a widespread revitalization that makes Harlem the neighborhood to watch.

SLEEK NEW AMERICAN CUISINE

**3  Commissary**

1030 Third Avenue

Matthew Kenney's newest restaurant takes his "C" theme to new uptown heights. Commissary, the successor to its two downtown sisters Canteen and Commune, has a sleek setting created by David Schefer Design using wraparound windows, black-stained floors and a polished white circular bar for dramatic emphasis. Pistachio and anise-crusted halibut, roasted cod glazed with vinegar and Riesling and tender venison chops paired with a juniper and celery-root gratin are just some of the Italian- and Asian-influenced dishes on Kenney's modern American menu. The bar area beneath the custom-designed chandelier is a great place to join flirty-somethings for an after-shopping Martini.

OLD MASTERS IN AN INTIMATE SETTING

**4  Frick Collection**

1 East 70th Street

This lavish mansion, the former home of the steel and railway tycoon Henry Clay Frick, houses a remarkable collection of paintings by all the weighty European masters. The intimate size of the museum, set back from Fifth Avenue by an elevated garden and a tranquil interior court planted with exotic palms, orchids and ferns and centered on an enormous fountain, make the Frick one of New York's most manageable and memorable museum experiences. Holbein's *Sir Thomas More*, Bellini's *St. Francis in the Desert* and Ingres's *Comtesse d'Hausonville* are just some of the treasures to behold in its four sumptuous rooms. Take a moment to look through the cast-iron gate from East 70th Street at the garden designed in 1977 by Russell Page. And, if you have time, wander up the leafy block towards the Asia Society (see right) for a tasting menu of architectural styles. The elegant houses that line this street range from an 1863 white-painted brownstone at no. 129 to an International Style edifice at no. 124, designed in 1940 by William Lescaze.

PAN-ASIAN ARTS

**5  Asia Society**

725 Park Avenue

Bartholomew Voorsanger is the architect of the reconfigured Asia Society on the corner of a verdant block of East 70th Street. He opened up the lobby and enclosed it partially in glass, then connected the building's four public floors with a free-floating staircase with white steel supports, blue laminated glass steps and light birch rails. The permanent gallery displays Korean ceramics, Indian miniatures, Japanese Buddhist paintings, Indonesian textiles and Thai sculptures, and the temporary exhibitions focus on various themes in pan-Asian culture. Be sure to stop awhile in the skylit Garden Court Café.

THE CLASSIC AMERICAN

**6  Ralph Lauren**

867 Madison Avenue

The mansion in which the Ralph Lauren fantasy world of WASPy privilege unfolds was originally designed in the 1890s for heiress Gertrude Rhinelander Waldo (who never actually moved in) by Kimball & Thompson. The 1980s renovation saved antique fixtures and original moldings. To amplify the aura of the leisure-filled lifestyle of a fictionalized prewar English gentility, the decorators added antique display furniture, Persian carpets, vintage riding boots, Vuitton trunks, cashmere upholstery, camel hair drapes, antique Baccarat chandeliers and Lalique panels.

AUCTION-HOUSE RESTAURANT

**7  Bid Brasserie**

1334 York Avenue

On the ground floor of the Richard Gluckman-designed New York headquarters of Sotheby's is a restaurant for dealers and collectors who've worked up an appetite on the auction floor. Dineen Nealy Architects have created a space that they describe as "clubby." Its laurel-wood walls showcase a revolving selection of art in a less formal context than that provided by the offices and galleries on the upper floors. The restaurant exudes an atmosphere of comfort, thanks in part to the muted color scheme and the use of soft materials, such as calfskin and chenille upholstery. The culinary emphasis is on contemporary American seasonal fare, and the prix-fixe menu might include braised lobster with corn relish, sautéed quail with bacon and salsify and gray sole with Manila clams and summer truffles.

**8 Cooper-Hewitt National Design Museum**

2 East 91st Street

The Cooper-Hewitt sits under the imperial umbrella of the Smithsonian Institution, and is the only museum in the United States devoted exclusively to historic and contemporary design. Its collections of 250,000 objects and exhibitions – such as "Rococo: The Continuing Curve 1730–2008" – are housed in the former home of industrial magnate, Andrew Carnegie. The sixty-four-room mansion, built from 1899 to 1902, is a challenging environment in which to present modern design, but its curators keep trying. The Arthur Ross Terrace and Garden, which is the scene of DJ sessions and many design-related gatherings in the summer, is a bucolic bonus to your visit.

THE MOTHER OF ALL MUSEUMS

**9 Metropolitan Museum of Art**

1000 Fifth Avenue

It's beyond huge. It's overwhelming. Even the long-distance runners among art lovers will need to take care to pace themselves in this venerable museum. Many of the Met's departments are extensive enough to be museums in themselves and it is advisable to treat them as such, one day at a time. The American Wing holds one of the most comprehensive collections of American painting and sculpture in the world. In the decorative arts section, seek out the Frank Lloyd Wright living room.

SANDWICHES AND SCULPTURE IN A ROOFSCAPE

**10 Iris and B. Gerald Cantor Roof Garden**

Metropolitan Museum of Art, 1000 Fifth Avenue

If you do nothing else, and providing it is some time between the month of May and late fall, you should ascend to the Iris and B. Gerald Cantor Roof Garden where, every year, a new sculpture show is installed. You can enjoy a sandwich and a drink and look over the treetops of Central Park as the sun dips behind them. A glorious finale to a day of art appreciation.

TIFFANY CENTERPIECE

**11 Seventh Regiment Armory**

643 Park Avenue

The venue for numerous art and antique fairs, this fantastical French medieval-style fortress is a treasure in itself. The Tiffany Room, encrusted with decorative stained glass, mosaic and metalwork, is the only existing example of Louis Comfort Tiffany's lavish interior design in the city. Upstairs is the Seventh Regiment Mess and Lounge, a faded 1950s time capsule of a restaurant.

MAGNET FOR BIBLIOPHILES

**12 Ursus Rare Books**

Carlyle Hotel, 981 Madison Avenue

A comprehensive selection of art reference books, superb copies of rare books in all fields and antique decorative prints can be found and browsed in this well-established store on the mezzanine of the Carlyle Hotel. Peter Kraus's collection is particularly strong in the areas of art, architecture, literature, travel and illustrated children's books. You might find a copy of *Alice in Wonderland* signed by Alice Liddell, or a first edition of Ludwig Bemelmans's *Madeline* to put you in the mood for the author and artist's namesake bar downstairs (see below).

CHILDHOOD MEMORIES IN A PIANO BAR

**13 Bemelmans Bar**

Carlyle Hotel, 35 East 76th Street

The walls of this dimly lit piano bar were painted by Ludwig Bemelmans, a 1940s Carlyle resident. The characters from his famous *Madeline* books are depicted in seasonal Central Park settings, and their whimsical charm provides a soothing backdrop for various sequestered celebrities and their afternoon cocktails.

HEAD FOR THE HEIGHTS

**14 Roosevelt Island Tramway + Guastavino's**

59th Street at Second Avenue and 409 East 59th Street

For one of the most spectacular views of New York – and at the mere price of a subway token – take a return trip on the Roosevelt Island Tramway. Built by the Swiss company Vonroll under designers Prentice & Chan and Ohlhausen, the aerial tramway has been used since 1976 to shuttle Roosevelt Island residents to and from Manhattan. During the four-minute ride, you are quietly whisked 250 feet (75 meters) above the East River, from where you can gaze up and down the water and along the high-rise canyons of Midtown. On your return you'll find sustenance in the monumental vaulted space beneath the Queensboro Bridge. Guastavino, British design guru Terence Conran's stylish restaurant, was created in collaboration with Hardy Holzman Pfeiffer Associates, who meticulously restored the ribbed-tile vaulting by Rafael Guastavino y Esposito.

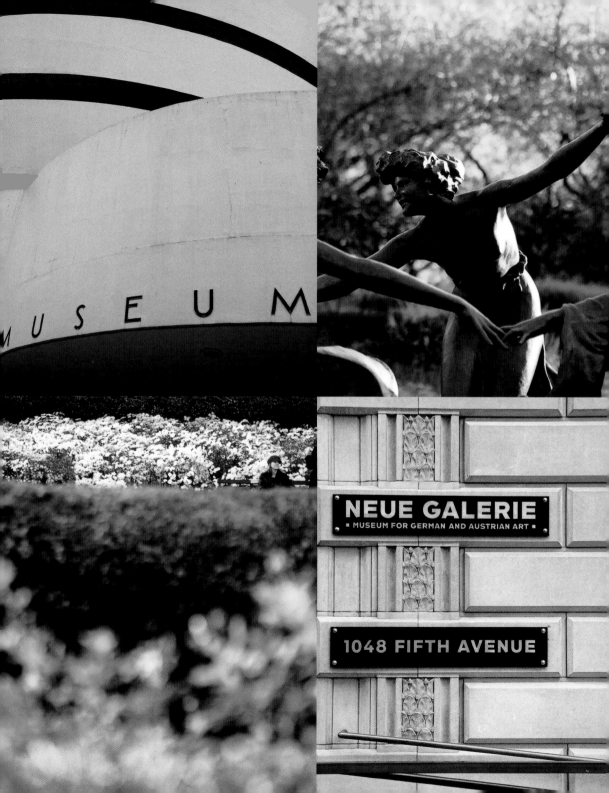

**15 Neue Galerie**

1048 Fifth Avenue

The collection of this small museum is dedicated to early 20th-century German and Austrian art. The original landmark building is a very fine mansion, dating from 1914, but it is the exquisitely restrained interior restoration at the hands of Annabelle Selldorf that will bring your applause. The paintings, sculptures and art objects stand out dramatically against Selldorf's quiet yet luminous environments. She has also isolated the major architectural features of the building, designed by John Merven Carrère and Thomas Hastings (see the New York Public Library; p. 68), so the spiraling marble and wrought-iron stair, the domed skylight and the marble and wood wainscoting can be appreciated.

**16 Café Sabarsky**

Neue Galerie, 1048 Fifth Avenue

Café Sabarsky is the Neue Galerie's excellent eatery, operated by Kurt Gutenbrunner, chef and owner of the acclaimed restaurant Wallsé. With its black and white tiled floor, lighting fixtures by Josef Hoffman, furniture by Adolf Loos and banquettes upholstered in an Otto Wagner fabric, Sabarsky draws inspiration from the Viennese cafés that were the centers of intellectual and artistic activity in the early 20th century. The menu focuses on traditional Austrian dishes and does not omit specialties such as strudel and Linzertorte.

**17 Guggenheim Museum**

1071 Fifth Avenue

Set amid the restrained and opulent apartment buildings that line Central Park's eastern side, Frank Lloyd Wright's fantastic white spiraling edifice edges into view as you walk up Fifth Avenue. Opened in 1959 to considerable excitement and controversy, the museum represents the high point of America's best-known modern architect. And if the building itself weren't enough reason to visit, the collection is outstanding. Coiling your way down from the top, you will encounter Peggy Guggenheim's trove of Cubist, Surrealist and Abstract Expressionist works and the outstanding photography collection that holds more than two hundred Robert Mapplethorpes. You will end up in the atrium below, where an impressive Friday night music program, often tied to the current exhibition, takes place.

**18 Conservatory Garden**

Central Park, Fifth Avenue at 105th Street

Central Park divides the two "Uppers," which tend to feel like estranged sisters. The people who live in these neighborhoods are fiercely loyal to their locale, so it is not uncommon to find people who have not gone to the "other side" for decades. The park itself is a design masterpiece. "Every foot of the park's surface, every tree and bush, as well as every arch, roadway and walk, has been placed where it is with a purpose," said its landscape architect, Frederick Law Olmsted. When, in 1857, the park began to be transformed from a dump and a bone-boiling plant into an urban idyll, it was surrounded only by open country and squatter shacks. The park's fringes were quickly developed, the biggest surge taking place between 1900 and 1920. Most of these buildings exhibit neo-Georgian, neo-Federal, neo-French or neo-Italian Renaissance styling. Aid your cultural digestion with a stroll through the symmetrical walks of the three formal gardens that constitute the Conservatory Gardens. These gardens – English, Italian and French – were added to Central Park's evolving grand plan in the 1930s, replacing the mouldering greenhouses established by the park's first gardener, Ignaz Pilat. Six acres (2.5 hectares) of hedges, canopied crab apple trees, beautifully manicured lawns, a trellis of wisteria, profusions of flowers, fountains and more await you in this seldom-visited corner of the park.

**19 72nd Street Subway**

Broadway at 72nd Street

Make your entrance to the Upper West Side via this Flemish Renaissance-style subway station control house, which occupies its own island at 72nd Street and Broadway. Designed in 1904 by Heins & Lafarge, it was restored in 2002 using the same materials as the original.

**20 Maxilla and Mandible**

451 Columbus Avenue

Just one block north of the American Museum of Natural History is a showroom where you can actually take the natural history exhibits home. Specimens from around the world, including bones and skeletons, fossils, eggs, insects, seashells, and the supplies necessary to their display can be found in this emporium of anatomical, paleontological, osteological and entomological oddities.

### 21 Zabar's

2245 Broadway

Even though you'll want to stop in your tracks and gaze around at the crazy interior of this New York institution, you'll be moved on by the sharp elbows of primarily Jewish shoppers focused intently on their purchases of handsliced nova, rye bread, challah and chicken pot pie. The smells of cheese, fresh bagels and ground coffee pull you up and down the aisles, on whose shelves imported packages of dried fruits and biscuits teeter perilously. This food bazaar gives you a real taste of New York.

SMOKED FISH AND HISTORY

### 22 Barney Greengrass

HISTORIC BOHEMIAN HAUNT

### 23 Café des Artistes

1 West 67th Street

For a perfect drink before a performance at Lincoln Center (see right), make your way to the hidden wood-paneled bar at the back of this romantic old-world restaurant. The neo-Gothic Hotel des Artistes was designed in 1917 by George Mort Pollard. The studio apartments did not have kitchens, but its tenants, although they were all artists, were hardly of the starving variety. They could congregate in the café, with its wraparound mural by Howard Chandler Christy of frolicking nude nymphs, for bistro food and conversation or send fresh ingredients to the kitchens via dumbwaiters and receive meals in return. Among the hotel's most famous residents were Isadora Duncan, Noël Coward, Rudolf Valentino and Norman Rockwell.

PRE-OPERA BISTRO

### 24 Café Luxembourg

200 West 70th Street

The 1980s take on an Art Deco interior includes a zinc bar, wicker chairs, black and white terrazzo floor and dairy wall tiles. The eclectic bistro menu is perfect for pre-opera grazing. Sit at the bar for some fried oysters and Champagne, elbow to elbow with discerning celebrities who weren't up for the trek ninety blocks south to the Odeon (p. 141).

CULTURAL MEGAPLEX

### 25 Lincoln Center for the Performing Arts

70 Lincoln Center Plaza

Even if you do not have tickets to see Plácido Domingo in *Andrea Chénier*, it is worth standing for a few moments at the center of this vast performing arts complex to soak up the urban scene. Bejeweled music- and ballet-lovers crisscross the plaza or wait for their dates on the edge of the central fountain. A variety of performance spaces were built in the late 1950s and 1960s by the architectural stars of the day, including Philip Johnson (state theater), Eero Saarinen (repertory theater) and Max Abramovitz (philharmonic hall). The Metropolitan Opera House, designed by Wallace K. Harrison in 1966 and featuring enormous paintings by Marc Chagall, is a spectacular venue in which to see a Met production under the artistic direction of James Levine.

WEST SIDE ELEGANCE

### 26 Dovetail

103 West 77th Street

Ensconced in a quiet townhouse mere feet away from the Natural History Museum, chef John Fraser serves witty riffs on American cuisine. Dovetail – named after an ingenious woodworker's joint that holds pieces of wood together without the use of nails – nails the balance between clever and delicious. Inside Richard Bloch's understated dining room, which combines the existing brick with sleek bird's-eye maple wood panels, Fraser serves classics like pistachio-crusted duck paired imaginatively with endive, caramelized apple and date purée. If it is just a burger and fries you're craving, try the Shake Shack, Danny Meyer's homage to the great American burger, just around the corner at Columbus and 77th Street. But for a soignée yet playful meal, Dovetail is your joint.

FOOD FOR THE SOUL

## 27 Sylvia's Soul Food Restaurant

328 Lenox Avenue (Malcolm X Boulevard)

For hot ribs, coconut cake and some Southern comfort, pop
into Sylvia's. Owners Sylvia and Herbert Woods, who met
in a South Carolina bean field when they were eleven
and twelve years old, married in 1944 and set up their
soul food restaurant in 1962. The restaurant has expanded
from an original capacity of thirty-five to fill almost an
entire block, but it remains a wholly African-American
owned and run business. Try the gospel lunch after Sunday
services at the Abyssinian Baptist Church (see below).

GOSPEL CHURCH

## 28 Abyssinian Baptist Church

132 Odell Clark Place

Built in 1923 by Charles W. Bolton, this blue-stone neo-
Gothic church is renowned for its late pastor, Adam Clayton
Powell, Jr., the first black congressman from New York
City. Services are at 9am and 11am on Sundays.

HARLEM JAZZ DEN

## 29 Lenox Lounge

288 Lenox Avenue (Malcolm X Boulevard)

This legendary lounge, specifically the Zebra room, has
played host to Billie Holiday, Miles Davis and John
Coltrane, among others. The original Art Deco interior with
zebra-striped walls, tiled floor and padded leather ceiling
has been restored, but the history of Harlem's premier jazz
venue (now that the Cotton Club and the Savoy Ballroom
have gone) still hangs in the air like smoke.

AFRICAN-AMERICAN ARTS

## 30 Studio Museum in Harlem

144 West 125th Street (Dr. Martin Luther King, Jr.
Boulevard)

The museum's unique focus on African-American art
and that of the African diaspora has produced some
groundbreaking exhibitions under the curatorial guidance
of curator Thelma Golden. Central to the museum's
mission is the challenging of canonical histories of
European and American modernism. The vibrant
artists-in-residence program produces regular showings
of emerging artists who work in the studio areas of
the building. For lunch at Sylvia's (see above) you need
only cross the street.

# Williamsburg
# Long Island City
# Dumbo

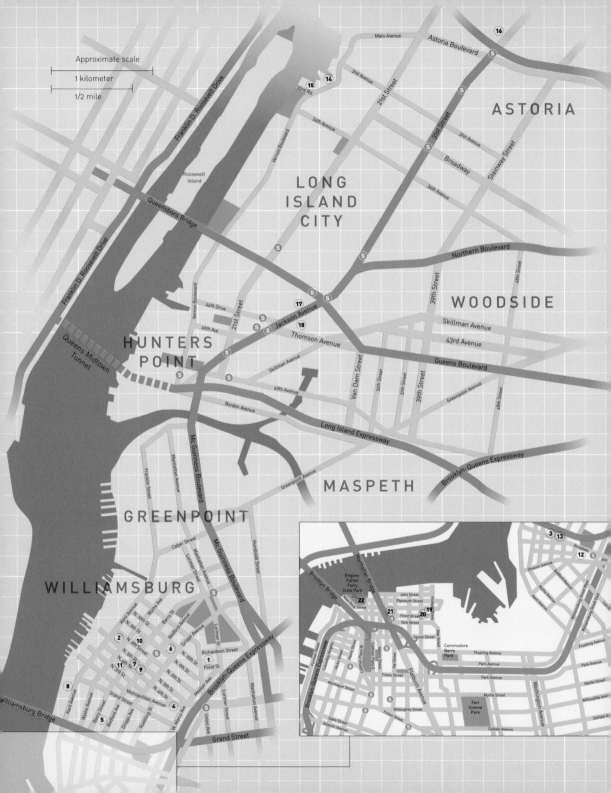

Approximate scale

1 kilometer

1/2 mile

ASTORIA

**16**

Main Avenue

Astoria Boulevard

31st Avenue

21st Street

31st Street

31st Avenue

**15** **14**

33rd Rd.

34th Avenue

Vernon Boulevard

Broadway

Steinway Street

Franklin D. Roosevelt Drive

LONG
ISLAND
CITY

34th Avenue

Roosevelt
Island

Queensboro Bridge

Northern Boulevard

46th Street

39th Street

WOODSIDE

Franklin D. Roosevelt Drive

44th Drive

44th Drive

21st Street

**17**

Jackson Avenue

**18**

Thomson Avenue

Skillman Avenue

43rd Avenue

Vernon Boulevard

46th Ave

Queens Midtown
Tunnel

HUNTERS
POINT

Skillman Avenue

Queens Boulevard

Van Dam Street

34th Street

37th Street

39th Street

Greenpoint Avenue

48th Street

49th Avenue

Borden Avenue

Long Island Expressway

Brooklyn-Queens Expressway

McGuinness Boulevard

Manhattan Avenue

Greenpoint Avenue

MASPETH

Franklin Street

Calyer Street

GREENPOINT

Humboldt Street

McGuinness Boulevard

Manhattan Avenue

Lorimer Street

WILLIAMSBURG

Kent Avenue

Wythe Ave

Berry St

Bedford Avenue

Driggs Avenue

Richardson Street

Frost St

Brooklyn-Queens Expressway

**2** **10**

N. 10th St

N. 9th St

**6**

N. 10th St

N. 9th St

**1**

**11** **7** **9**

N. 8th St

N. 7th St

N. 6th St

Metropolitan Avenue

Lorimer Street

Manhattan Avenue

**8**

N. 3rd St

Grand Street

Kent Avenue

Wythe Avenue

Berry Street

Bedford Street

Driggs Ave

Roebling St

W. Marcy Ave

**4**

Williamsburg Bridge

**5**

Union Ave

Grand Street

---

Manhattan Bridge

**3** **13**

Broadway

Division Avenue

**12**

Brooklyn Bridge

Empire-
Fulton
Ferry
State Park

John Street

Plymouth Street

**19**

**22**

New Dock Street

**21**

Front Street

**20**

York Street

Sands Street

Commodore
Barry
Park

Flushing Avenue

Park Avenue

Brooklyn-Queens Expressway

Columbia Street

Navy Street

Adams Street E.

Clinton Street E.

Flatbush Avenue

Park Avenue

Washington Avenue

Myrtle Street

Montague Street

Tillary Street

Fort
Greene
Park

Myrtle Street

Willoughby Avenue

State Street

Willoughby Street

Fulton Street

Atlantic Street

DeKalb Avenue

With what to locals seems like improbable velocity, the Brooklyn neighborhood of Williamsburg has in a few short years transformed itself from a declining industrial district into an artists' enclave and hipster destination. In the mid-1800s Williamsburg was a fashionable resort area, attracting industrialists and professionals, with hotels, clubs and beer gardens clustered around the Brooklyn ferry park. Once the Williamsburg Bridge was opened, the neighborhood became increasingly industrialized; Williamsburg native Henry Miller remembered "the ironworks where the red furnace glowed and men walked toward the glowing pit with huge shovels in their hands" of the 1890s. At that time the waterfront was cluttered with docks, shipyards, warehouses, taverns, mills and breweries. Today there are fewer than 9,000 manufacturing jobs (compared to 93,000 in 1961).

Fortunately, there is still enough of an eclectic ethnic mix of Puerto Ricans, Poles and Hasidim to prevent the burgeoning scene from becoming too homogeneous. Thanks to the idiosyncratic shops and relaxed attitude, on weekday afternoons the area has a quiet, almost villagelike, atmosphere. But already many of the artists who forged the way in the early 1990s have been priced out of the lofts they once squatted. As yet there is no hotel in the neighborhood, so stay in Manhattan and take the L-train three stops from Union Square. Bedford Avenue, the main drag, and the streets between North 9th Street and Broadway that cross it, are dotted with enough boutiques, antiques shops, galleries, cafés, restaurants and bars to keep you happily occupied for an afternoon that may well turn into night.

Several miles to the north of Williamsburg, in the sprawling borough of Queens (which has, until now, remained a frontier to most Manhattanites), Long Island City is another windswept industrial zone that is undergoing revitalization thanks to a growing art, film and design community. New York seems to have fixed its greedy gaze on the neighborhood, with its residential pockets of Asian and Latin American immigrants. The advance guard has already installed itself in choice lofts, and it may not be long before Long Island City, just like Williamsburg, has its corner bodegas turned into cappuccino-serving cafés playing electronica. In the area between the Manhattan and Brooklyn Bridges, known as Dumbo (or Down Under the Manhattan Bridge Overpass), the 19th-century brick warehouses are dense with the workshops and studios of artists and designers. With real estate development in full swing, a Starbucks already in place and a growing contingent of home furnishings boutiques and cafés, it looks as if the artists will soon be going the way of the longshoremen who previously populated the area.

LOCAL COLOR

**1 Pete's Candy Store**

709 Lorimer Street

You will discover the real charm of this old-fashioned bar, set in a 1900s brick storefront, in the narrow, curtained-off back room, which features an upholstered vaudeville stage lit with vanity bulbs. The room, padded like the interior of a jewel box, hosts nightly performances by local bluegrass bands and poets, booked by co-owner Juliana Nash. Bingo and quiz nights on Tuesdays and Wednesdays are wildly popular with the vintage T-shirt and truckers-cap set.

BUILT BY YOU

**2 Built By Wendy**

46 North 6th Street

Once a record-store clerk, Wendy Mullin started off in 1991 designing hand-tooled guitar straps. Soon, however, Mullin expanded her range to include all-American dresses, jeans and T-shirts. In her small Williamsburg boutique, opened in 2005, Mullin offers whimsical designs – like a silk dress inspired by *The Red Balloon* and T-shirts with illustrations of the *Bad News Bears* on them – and the skinny-legged jeans found on the skinny-legged hipsters who roam Bedford Avenue. For the crafty, she also offers Built By You patterns so that you can sew your own Built By Wendy creation in the comfort of your own home. Another store is in Little Italy (7 Centre Market Place).

DINER STYLE

**3 Diner**

138

EAT AT THE FAT PIG

**4 Fette Sau**

139

EMERGING TENDENCIES

**5 Momenta Art**

359 Bedford Avenue

Momenta Art is a nonprofit exhibition space directed by artist Eric Heist. Its two-person shows, with a bias toward American artists, and its thematic exhibits such as "Pop Patriotism," curated in response to the national surge of flag-waving after 9/11, are consistently thought-provoking. For each exhibition in this pristine white box of a space, the gallery publishes a newsletter that includes information about the artists and their works.

AT THE VANGUARD

**6 Pierogi 2000**

177 North 9th Street

The name of this gallery, one of the most established in the neighborhood, is a reference to the dumpling favored by the vicinity's Polish residents. Pierogi 2000 has monthly shows featuring the work of artists from Williamsburg, Brooklyn, and beyond. You can riffle through samples of work from more than 500 mostly American artists, as long as you don the white gloves provided. The original unframed works stored in flat files are affordable and include the work of such notables as Lawrence Weiner, Keith Tyson and Bob and Roberta Smith.

BISCUITS 'N' GRAVY

**7 Egg**

135 North 5th Street

Egg has no sign, but you can tell where this brunch spot is by the swarm of Williamsburg residents standing outside, stamping their feet in winter and wiping their foreheads in summer. The owner, George Weld, a native North Carolinian, imported his knowledge of fried chicken and biscuits to the epicenter of irony and has met an unquenchable demand. Even hipsters need brunch. Now the perpetually packed restaurant – Spartan to the point of barren – keeps all-day brisk business, serving heaping portions of biscuits and gravy and crispy, succulent salty chicken pieces. In 2008, Weld bought a farm in Upstate New York from which he harvests much of what is found on Egg's menu.

WAREHOUSE HAPPENINGS

**8 Glasslands Gallery**

289 Kent Avenue

On a desolate block of industrial warehouses in the looming shadow of the deserted Domino Sugar Factory, an unremarkable door leads into a remarkable space. More accurately, the space itself isn't that remarkable, rather it is how it is filled. Started in 2006 by artists Brooke Baxter and Rolyn Hu, Glasslands Gallery regularly hosts up-and-coming garage rock bands like the Beachnicks, more established acts like Sonic Youth's Thurston Moore, and raging all-night brass band-fueled dance parties, as well as more traditional art shows in an old warehouse space where it seems anything goes and anything can happen.

INDEPENDENT BOOKSTORE

## 9 Spoonbill & Sugartown

218 Bedford Avenue

Located in the Real Form Girdle Building, smack in the center of Williamsburg's thoroughfare of cool, Spoonbill & Sugartown restores your confidence in the survival of the independent bookstore. Specializing in used, rare and new books on contemporary art, art history, architecture and design, the store numbers among its staff some large sleepy cats that drape themselves over the piles of volumes waiting to be shelved.

OLD FOR NEW

## 10 Future Perfect

VIENNA ON THE EAST RIVER

## 11 Radegast

113 North 3rd Street

In 2007, Williamsburg was the Ground Zero of New York's cultural renaissance, and in dire need of a Bohemian beer hall (so many bohemians, not enough beer). Ivan Aohut, owner of the original Bohemian Hall & Beer Garden (p. 157) in Astoria, Queens, remedied the problem by converting two old warehouses into a little bit of Vienna on the East River. With Czech designer Jirka Kolar and lumber from a 150-year-old barn, the team recreated a faithful turn-of-the-century *Bierhaus*, down to the peeling murals of Kaiser Wilhelm II glowering down from the wall. Anachronistically but fortuitously, there's also a retractable glass roof. During the warmer months, bearded hipsters crowd around the long communal tables and log benches underneath the starry sky. The din of good-natured beer-fueled banter, the endless hiss of Hoftbrau sausage on the grill, and nightly live music make this former candy warehouse seem like the last vestige of the Austro-Hungarian empire.

BIKERS' BAR

## 12 Moto

394 Broadway

Motorbike enthusiasts Billy Phelps and John McCormick converted a decrepit check-cashing joint into a motorcycle-themed no-frills bar with a snacking menu. Situated in the Jewish-meets-Puerto Rican community of south Williamsburg, the bar prefigures the imminent southward development of the neighborhood.

CONTEMPORARY VINTAGE

## 13 Dressler
149 Broadway

Working from the original 1910 tile floor, interior designer Joseph Foglia built this elegant restaurant from the ground up. "I wanted to create a place inspired by classic New York," he says, "but which used the newest technology." The aluminum chandeliers might seem vintage, but on closer inspection the filigree silhouettes turn out to be intricately carved with a water-jet cutting machine. The custom-made stools appear as if they wouldn't be out of place at a 1920s speakeasy, until, that is, you notice they are tricked out with cartoon characters. The interior is the perfect complement to chef Polo Dobkin's nouvelle cuisine, which strives to make the old new again. Standout dishes on the seasonal menu include a cider-braised pork shank, accompanied by lemon meringue tart with a strangely compelling green tea anglaise.

ART BY THE RIVER

## 14 Socrates Sculpture Park
Broadway and Vernon Boulevard

Set on the Long Island City bank of the East River with Midtown high-rises as a backdrop, this outdoor sculpture park is the site of large-scale works by both emerging and recognized artists. Socrates Sculpture Park was an abandoned riverside landfill and illegal dump site until 1986, when a coalition of artists and community members, under the leadership of artist Mark di Suvero, transformed the land into an open studio and exhibition space and a neighborhood park for local residents. Exhibitions rotate on a semi-annual basis; a visit to the park a month or two preceding an opening allows a glimpse into the sculpture-making process.

SCULPTED TRANQUILITY

## 15 Isamu Noguchi Garden Museum
9–01 33rd Road

Thirteen indoor and outdoor galleries within a converted factory building encircle a tranquil garden containing Isamu Noguchi's granite and basalt sculptures. The factory was the studio and storage facility of the Japanese sculptor and designer of furniture, stage sets and public spaces. On exhibition are more than 240 of Noguchi's works, including stone, metal, wood, and clay sculptures, and models for public projects and dance sets. His Akari light sculptures are for sale in the museum store-café, enabling you to take a piece of Zen home with you.

**16 Bohemian Hall & Beer Garden**

**17 P.S.1 Contemporary Art Center**

22–25 Jackson Avenue

The corridors of the converted Public School No. 1 now echo with the clickety-clack of Prada-heeled contemporary art lovers. Be sure to seek out the James Turrell Room at dusk for a sublime encounter with a square-shaped patch of shifting sky. And for non-claustrophobes, find Robert Wogan's fourth-floor installation, a pitch-black passageway that narrows until ejecting you into a pyramid-shaped room showing a video of the pre-renovation P.S.1. Each year the courtyard is transformed into an urban playground by an emerging architect. The installation, usually water-themed, sets the scene for Saturday afternoon DJ Warm Up sessions.

**18 SculptureCenter**

44–19 Purves Street

SculptureCenter, which has been around since 1928, today inhabits a former Long Island City trolley repair shop that was redesigned in 2002 by Maya Lin, the artist responsible for the Vietnam Veterans Memorial in Washington, DC. With more than 9,000 square feet (836 square meters) of interior and outdoor exhibition space and an innovative curatorial policy, the center provides an important forum for the conceptual, aesthetic and material concerns of contemporary sculpture, as well as staging solo exhibitions of such artists as Petah Coyne and Rita McBride.

**19 Vinegar Hill House**

72 Hudson Avenue

The strip of colonial houses abutting the Brooklyn Navy Yard is one of the oldest neighborhoods in the borough (see Vinegar Hill; right). This former red-light district was a largely forgotten cobblestone byway until a couple of Freeman's (p. 137) alumni opened up Vinegar Hill House in a former ice-cream parlor. The interior boasts a colonial flag on one wall and a pipe organ on the other, and the crowd is a mix of locals and the more adventurous of the Manhattan hipsters. The locally sourced menu is full of home-style favorites like roast cod and a chocolate cake made with Guinness and cream-cheese frosting.

**20 Vinegar Hill**

Between Hudson and Gold Streets

Cut off from the rest of the world by the Brooklyn Navy Yard on one side and the smokestacks of a power plant on the other, Vinegar Hill is an eight-square-block of row houses and lush dooryards that evoke mid-19th-century Brooklyn. Wander the Belgian-block streets lined with charmingly disheveled brownstones, their storefront windows bearing traces of their former commercial lives.

**21 Spring**

126a Front Street

Dumbo's converted industrial buildings contain warrens of artists' studios and design workshops. Some of the resulting artwork can be viewed and purchased at the innovative gallery Spring, or "three-dimensional magazine," as the owners, textile designer Steve Butcher and producer Anna Cosentino, refer to it.

**22 Jacques Torres**

66 Water Street

One of the true pleasures of visiting Dumbo is going to the charming Jacques Torres chocolate boutique, picking out a selection of delicious chocolates patterned with red and gold motifs, and having them boxed in the immaculate packaging. If it's cold, stay for a cup of hot chocolate so thick you can stand your spoon up in it. Otherwise, take your purchases to Brooklyn Bridge Park (also home to the picturesque 1890 Tobacco Inspection Warehouse) and drink in the unsurpassed views of Manhattan.

**23 Zakka**

155 Plymouth Street

This store-and-gallery destination, now relocated to Dumbo from SoHo, features an immaculate selection of graphic art books, as well as clothing, music and stationery. The owner takes particular delight in products of the Japanese subculture and art scene, but Zakka also carries an international mix of titles and brands. Among the most sought-after publications are *Gas Book*, *Stash* and *Idea* magazine, while popular toys include the Kaws series of Companions and Mumbleboy's stuffed dolls.

# Park Slope
# Smith Street
# Fort Greene

"No! Sleep! Till Brooklyn!" The Beastie Boys' rallying cry may have made sense in 1990, but today Brooklyn has enough going on to keep you up all night. Several of its neighborhoods – Dumbo, Smith Street, Fort Greene and Red Hook among them – are sprouting new scenes that have earned them multiple stars on New York's style map. The fastest developing destination territories tend, unsurprisingly, to be clustered near the three bridges that connect Brooklyn to Lower Manhattan.

Park Slope is the older hippie sister of the bunch. If it doesn't already, it should be able to lay claim to having the largest number of baby strollers per block of anywhere in the nation. It's impossible to carry your decaf soy cappuccino more than a few Birkenstock-shod feet without bumping into another set of proud young parents, often same-sex. The charming brownstones and mansions of this district were built around Prospect Park's Manhattan-facing aspect in the late 1800s after it opened its gates and the Brooklyn Bridge was completed.

Brooklyn's most happening scene is acted out on a section of Smith Street that has its head in Boerum Hill – a neighborhood of brownstones with prices kept in check by the proximity of the projects – and its tail in the Italianate Carroll Gardens. Until the late 1990s, when urban renewal paved the way for pioneering restaurants such as Patois (at no. 255), this stretch of Smith was a no-go zone. Now the street is peopled by shoppers and diners a few years older and some degrees less fashion-obsessed than those found on its rival, Williamsburg's Bedford Avenue. By day you can browse the vintage boutiques and furniture stores that double as cafés, and by night dine on bistro fare at Café Luluc (no. 214) or Bar Tabac (no. 128), or on more sophisticated cuisine at Grocery (no. 288). Drinking venues range from nicotine-stained classics, such as the Brooklyn Inn (p. 106), to the contemporary good looks of Bar Below (no. 209).

The popular image of Fort Greene is one colored by Spike Lee's famously bittersweet portrayals of the artsy, well-educated African-American district in which he came of age. And while the historic district of Fort Greene – with its luscious late-19th-century brownstones that line the streets to the south and east of Fort Greene Park, named for its pivotal role in the Revolutionary War – is still characterized by the racial and economic diversity that Lee documented, the nightlife around Lafayette and DeKalb Avenues is an utterly contemporary phenomenon. French bistros such as Loulou, Chez Oscar, Ici and Liquors cater to the crowds who throng to the Brooklyn Academy of Music (p. 109) and the ever-increasing local population of young professionals, who reap the benefits of an area rich in black culture.

**1  Bed and Breakfast on the Park**

114

HORTICULTURAL TREASURE

**2  Brooklyn Botanic Garden**

1000 Washington Avenue

Known for its annual Cherry Blossom Festival, the Brooklyn Botanic Garden is among the best-regarded in the country. Stroll beneath wisteria-laden trellises to the rose garden boasting 1,200 different varieties. The recently restored Japanese garden features a teahouse overlooking a pond seething with turtles and giant koi. A blue heron, a frequent visitor to the pond, completes the tranquil scene. The greenhouses contain one of the world's largest collections of bonsai trees, some well over 100 years old. Founded in 1910, the Brooklyn Botanic Garden has far more charm than its larger counterpart in the Bronx.

ART AT THE PARK

**3  Brooklyn Museum**

200 Eastern Parkway

The Brooklyn Museum is the second largest art museum in the city and one of the largest in the US. Although acquiring a certain notoriety following the withdrawal of funding for the 1999 "Sensation" exhibition, the museum boasts a magnificent permanent collection, which includes more than a million objects, ranging from Ancient Egypt to contemporary America. The façade of the 19th-century Beaux Arts building has been recently renovated, and has acquired a new entrance pavilion. Music and entertainment programs take place on the first Saturday of each month.

UP, UP AND AWAY

**4  Brooklyn Superhero Supply Co.**

372 Fifth Avenue

If Superman ever ripped his cape or The Spirit misplaced his mask, they would head straight for the Brooklyn Superhero Supply Co., where capes, invisibility paint, grappling hooks, and all the prerequisites of superheroism are on sale. The shelves are fully stocked with products like Antimatter: In a Recyclable Steel Can, a can of Time Travel for $14, and the Speed of Light in what appears to be a thermos. But the store is simply a Clark Kent cover for a more important purpose. The real heroes of the store are found in the back room, accessible by a secret bookshelf door. There volunteers for writer Dave Eggers' nonprofit

foundation 826NYC tutor children between the ages of six to eighteen in expository writing. Surely there and in the front, the sign (also for sale) reading "The vow of heroism is not to be taken lightly" is heeded.

WHISKEY PALACE

**5  Char No. 4**

157

SECRET PASSAGE TO INDIA

**6  Layla**

86 Hoyt Street

Assembled in this diminutive store are exotically hued textiles, home furnishings, gold chandelier earrings, and clothing handpicked from India, Turkey and Lebanon.

BURNISHED BAR

**7  Brooklyn Inn**

148 Hoyt Street

A classic old-time Brooklyn establishment dating from 1868, the inn features a large ornate antique bar, huge mirrors and a high tin ceiling. During the day, light streams in through the dusty windows to fall on the open notebooks and discarded pens of the hard-drinking regulars, who seem to include a disproportionate number of writers. Argue about Kierkegaard or play a neighborly game of pool in the back room. At night, the place can fill up with young professionals back from a hard day in "the city." With only a neon Pilsner Urquell sign on its neo-Gothic iron-and-wood exterior, you'll need to follow the locals to find this corner spot.

WINE AND CHEESE

**8  Sherwood Café at Robin des Bois**

153

DUDS FOR DUDES

**9  Watts on Smith**

248 Smith Street

Husband-and-wife team Jennifer Argenta and Anthony Nelson offer Brooklyn boys a selection of labels that range from such UK style staples as Duffer St. George and Ben Sherman to sporty American favorites like Original Penguin and Fred Perry.

WORLD'S BEST CHEESECAKE

**10 Junior's**

386 Flatbush Avenue

From the day Harry Rosen opened Junior's on Flatbush Avenue in 1950, three generations of his family have been baking "the world's most fabulous cheesecakes" and mixing egg creams for locals and those who venture across the Manhattan Bridge. The flashing lights of its signage are particularly photogenic.

THE SOUL OF JAZZ

**11 Frank's Cocktail Lounge**

660 Fulton Street

Any single aspect of this bar, when taken alone, would be uninspired: shabby carpet, low ceiling, dark wall paneling. But to go to Frank's on a Thursday, when Lonnie Youngblood is blowing his saxophone and the old-timers are holding court, is to be transported back in time to a Fort Greene that existed before Spike Lee and the Notorious B.I.G., and to feel the soul behind what would become the hip-hop heart of New York.

PERFORMANCES ON THE EDGE

**12 Brooklyn Academy of Music**

30 Lafayette Avenue

This recently restored 19th-century building, the cultural cornerstone of Fort Greene, stages an eclectic mix of opera, dance and experimental performances by the likes of Lou Reed, Philip Glass and Laurie Anderson. BAM, as it is known, also houses BAM Rose Cinemas, arguably the best movie theater in New York. Apart from the regular seasonal performances, BAM also hosts several festivals, including the feted Next Wave Festival, begun in 1983.

VIENNESE WALTZ

**13 Thomas Beisl**

25 Lafayette Avenue

Until the BAM restaurant is bestowed a much-needed overhaul, Academy visitors are advised to go across the road to Thomas Beisl for pre-show appetizers or post-show desserts. Celebrated Austrian chef-owner Thomas Ferlesch left Café des Artistes (p. 86) to renovate this location into a bistro. A liver terrine with kumquat-cranberry compote, speck and sausage charcuterie, and an inexpensive cheese plate make excellent snacks, while heartier appetites are satiated with beef cheek goulash and schnitzel.

# Style Traveler

sleep • eat • drink
shop • retreat

# sleep

The days of $1,000-a-night hotels are over, and good riddance. New Yorkers have always had the ability to make more with less, and hoteliers have taken up the challenge. A new crop of boutique hotels have harnessed this minimalist and economical approach, while keeping intact the luxurious escapism. Hoteliers-of-the-moment Eric Goode and Sean MacPherson have turned a flophouse into The Jane, one of the city's most exciting new hotels, while Robert De Niro et al have imported an antique Japanese teahouse into the basement of Tribeca's Greenwich Hotel. Necessity is the mother of invention, they say. It's also the mother of a good night's sleep.

## Bed and Breakfast on the Park

113 Prospect Park West, Brooklyn
Rooms from $155

Prospect Park, Frederick Law Olmsted and Calvert Vaux's 1873 vision of a bucolic idyll, provides 536 acres (217 hectares) of leafy respite for overtaxed Brooklynites. On its west side, beyond the 90-acre (36-hectare) greensward known as the Long Meadow, and at the crown of the slope that runs down through the villagelike neighborhood of Park Slope, is Prospect Park West. The mansions that still grace this avenue were erected in the late 1880s, shortly after the completion of the Brooklyn Bridge enabled easier access to Manhattan. Number 113, a four-story brownstone built in 1892, is one of Brooklyn's top ten landmarks of Victorian architecture. Refashioned in 1987 into a bed and breakfast, it has nine rooms, some with views all the way to the Statue of Liberty and those at the front overlooking the park.

Owner Liana Paolella, an antiques dealer as well as innkeeper, has furnished the brownstone with her wares, which range in date from the mid-19th to the early 20th centuries, and include some especially fine oil paintings from her family collection. The original moldings in the parlor are of intricately carved oak, African mahogany and bird's-eye maple. The suite on the top floor has a double canopy bed swathed in French lace, a large antique bath, a sitting area and a private rooftop garden with views of the Manhattan skyline. Breakfast is taken in the Victorian dining room, pooled with colored light from the stained-glass bay windows. A feast consisting of homemade bread, German pancakes, crêpes, quiche Lorraine and homemade jams and jellies is spread out on the huge table, set with Irish linen, Royal Crown Derby and Waterford jars. Rest assured that you will be well fed for your exploration of the nearby Brooklyn "villages" of Park Slope, Fort Greene and Boerum Hill.

## Greenwich Hotel

377 Greenwich Street
Rooms from $475

The actor Robert De Niro is the undisputed king of Tribeca, having founded the Tribeca Film Festival, among other claims to fame. So it makes sense that he is a partner at the Greenwich Hotel, the neighborhood's most stylish accommodation. The 88-room hotel is an artful mélange of influences. Old and new, East and West, commingle in the Samantha Crasco-designed rooms. High-end yet Spartan, with reclaimed chestnut floors and bright Moroccan tiles in the bathrooms, the Greenwich is an antidote to the stuffy settees of other (uptown) hotels. The public spaces, which include a private courtyard beset on all sides by cascading ivy and a "drawing room" covered in Turkish travertine marble, remind guests of an Italian palazzo. But it is the Shibui Spa and pool, both designed by Mikio Shinagawa, using craftspeople and materials from Japan, in the hotel's basement which are really marvelous. The lantern-lit pool is surrounded by a transported 250-year-old Japanese wooden farmhouse that was assembled by a team of craftsmen using wooden joints and an ancient knot-tying technique. Not a nail was used – the Greenwich is much too classy and refined for that sort of thing.

## City Club Hotel

**30** 55 West 44th Street
Rooms from $289

The opening of the City Club Hotel signaled the beginning of a new era of what shall henceforth be known as post-boutiquism. Jeff Klein, a worldly socialite and first-time hotelier, dubs his refined travelers' haven an "anti-boutique" hotel, with an "anti-lobby" to match. Indeed, in contrast to the wonderland that welcomes guests into the Royalton across the road, this lobby is intentionally small and cozy. With its red coffee table piled high with books and vases of orchids, waxed cork flooring and pillow-strewn window seat, it feels more like the entrance to a private residence than to a 65-room hotel in Manhattan's theater district. Interior designer Jeffrey Bilhuber has erred on the side of eclectic aestheticism. In the mezzanine lounge, Queen Anne chairs abut Brancusi stools, while a Fabien Baron mobile offsets vintage framed playbills. Bilhuber's blend of traditional and modern sensibilities is played out with impeccable restraint in the guestrooms. The bathrooms are of chocolate-colored marble and nickel chrome, the walls are finished to simulate hand-corrugated plaster; the furniture is Honduran mahogany, and the selection of quirky ornaments has been distinctively curated. And, lest one begin to feel that it's all about style, the details add a dose of tangible luxury, such as the television with a mirror screen that dissolves once turned on. All of this adds up to a contemporary version of the comfort once provided by the building's original occupant: a 1904 gentlemen's club.

You approach this small, secretive hotel – formed by the joining of two 1830s townhouses – by a flight of steep steps from the sidewalk to the parlor floor. To the left as you enter is Lady Mendl's, a tea salon furnished with antiques and serving a five-course high tea with sandwiches of the thinly sliced cucumber and smoked-salmon variety. The dozen atmospheric guestrooms, restored by owner Naomi Blumenthal with Larry Wente in 1994, feature fireplaces (non-working, unfortunately, but there is a blazing fire in the parlor during winter months) and hardwood floors. They are furnished with period armoires, four-poster brass beds, Oriental rugs and antique lighting fixtures. While some have likened the experience of a night at the Inn to a stay with an eccentric great-aunt, the bed and breakfast has far more romantic potential than such a comparison evokes. The Madame Olenska suite – named in homage to Edith Wharton, who once lived in nearby Gramercy Square – is the largest in the hotel. It boasts a window seat overlooking Irving Place, an antique typewriter, and a sitting room in which to take your complimentary continental breakfast and the *New York Times,* or to receive visitors. Every bathroom features an early 20th-century pedestal sink and brass fixtures. And though such luxury might tempt you to stay in your claw-foot tub with a copy of *The Age of Innocence*, observation of more contemporary manners can be found a short walk in any direction from the hotel's front door. A few blocks to the southwest is Union Square, originally constructed in 1831 and now home to the bustling Greenmarket (p. 54) above ground, and a major subway hub below. Take the L-train three stops toward Brooklyn to explore the city's hippest neighborhood and most vibrant emerging art scene, Williamsburg.

50 **Thompson Lower East Side**

1 190 Allen Street
Rooms from $179

There was a real danger that hotelier Jason Pomeranc's slick version of cool would look out of place amid the gritty edginess of the Lower East Side. Thankfully, though his new hotel may look like a take on the National Security Agency building, courtesy of architect Ed Rawlings's tinted glass façade, there are enough touches to make it fit right in. Inside the 141 spacious guestrooms, the abstract photographs by legendary artist Lee Friedlander have been formed into lightboxes, which are mounted above the low minimalist beds. (Don't worry, they can be turned off.) From underneath the water of the third-floor pool, tiles etched with Andy Warhol's face stare up at you. The restaurant, a highly rated haute pan-Asian venture called Shang and run by noted chef Susur Lee, is dominated not only by gigantic gold lanterns, but also by the work of abstract artist Peter Halley. In fact, it's hard to escape the fashionista art world even if you wanted to. Even the hotel staff wear uniforms designed by Rogan. Art–fashion nexuses notwithstanding, there is plenty else to commend the hotel. Among many temptations, the bathrooms are stocked with Kiehl's (p. 169) products, the sheets are by Sferra, and the view is panoramic.

**The Jane** `32`

`9` 113 Jane Street

Rooms from $150

New York's best stories are those of redemption, and The Jane hotel, a new boutique property on the far West Side, is a tale of being lost and then found. For years the beautiful building, built in 1908 by Ellis Island's architect William Boring, languished as a YMCA, and then simply as a flophouse. Behind the bricks of the elegant neoclassical façade, the 211 tiny rooms were occupied by vagrants and drug addicts. Then in 2007, Eric Goode and Sean MacPherson, the design duo behind the Bowery (p. 130) and Maritime hotels, as well as funky cocktail lounge The Park (p. 152), bought the building and began restoring it to its former glory. There are 150 tiny "cabin rooms" and fifty larger ones dispersed over four floors and among the still inhabited rooms of pre-hotel tenants. The "captain's quarters" are spare, but accommodate a queen-sized bed and bathroom. The cabin rooms barely fit one person, let alone a bathroom, which is to be found at the end of the hall. But the rooms are elegant and stylish – and recommended. Goode spent years sourcing the anigre paneling and finding the perfect mod-orange comforters. A night at The Jane is a bit like sleeping in a first-class train compartment. The Jane "isn't for everyone," says Goode; there's Wi-Fi, for example, but no restaurant. A list of nearby delis, however, is provided.

**The Lowell**

28 East 63rd Street
Rooms from $575

Scandinavian down comforters, Chinese porcelains, 18th-century prints, Fauchon and Dean & Deluca goodies in the minibars, and Bulgari amenities in the marble bathrooms – the guestrooms of The Lowell exude uptown luxury from every Frette linen pore. The suites, boasting wood fires, libraries and terraces, are even more sumptuous. Its discreet location on tree-lined East 63rd Street in the Upper East Side Historic District and its immaculate service endear this hotel to a privacy-seeking clientele. Originally an apartment hotel of one- and two-bedroom suites, designed in the late 1920s by Henry Stern Churchill, The Lowell is now a landmark building. The exterior of the lower floors features a mosaic façade of brick and glazed terracotta; higher up is a series of asymmetrical terraced setbacks. The gorgeous lobby, designed by Dalmar Tift III, is comprised of Art Deco details, French Empire-style furniture, chiaroscuro walls and a rare desk console signed by Edgar Brandt. The slightly too exquisite chintz of the hotel's furnishings may not suit all tastes, but if you like your country cottages one block from Central Park and within walking distance of all the uptown museums and Madison Avenue boutiques, The Lowell will be your whimsical nirvana.

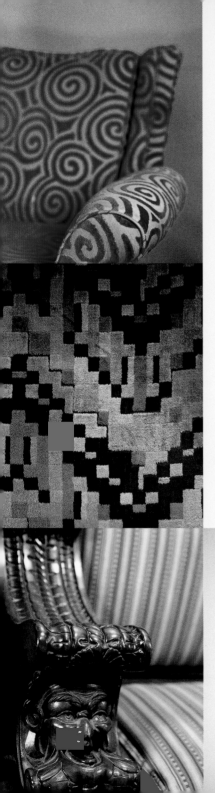

## 32 **Hotel Chelsea**

**20** 222 West 23rd Street
Rooms from $169

Legends of the Hotel Chelsea loom even larger than the imposing Victorian-Gothic edifice that dominates much of the block between Seventh and Eighth Avenues on 23rd Street. Apart from the more dramatic scenes that have colored its rooms and corridors – from Nancy Spungen's stabbing at the hands of boyfriend Sid Vicious in Room 100 to Dylan Thomas's last drink in 205 – the hotel's guest register is a veritable index of 20th-century American literature. Long-term tenants have included Mark Twain, Tennessee Williams, Arthur Miller and O. Henry; Arthur Clarke penned *2001: A Space Odyssey* here, and William S. Burroughs wrote *Naked Lunch* within its walls. But the hotel's location within the city's gallery district and its residents, including Jim Dine, Claes Oldenburg and Andy Warhol's Chelsea Girls, have earned it the dubious distinction of being named the sleeping quarters for the art world – albeit for those with a rock 'n' roll rather than MoMA-inspired interpretation of art. Holly Solomon had a gallery in Room 425, and the lobby doubles as a gallery showing the work of previous residents, some of whom purportedly paid for their lodging in kind. Since 2001, a far less down-and-out clientele can be found under the hotel's canopy as they line up for entrance to velvet-roped Serena, a swanky subterranean cocktail bar named for its owner, a well-known New York caterer. The Chelsea's red-brick façade and lacy wrought-iron balconies are the work of Hubert Pirsson & Co., who built the hotel in 1884 as the city's first cooperative apartment complex. Be warned that seedy cool is apt to teeter dangerously over the edge to downright dingy. But if, like Leonard Cohen, writer of the song "Chelsea Hotel #2," you "love hotels to which, at 4am, you can bring along a midget, a bear and four ladies, drag them to your room and no one cares about it at all," then you'll feel right at home.

ECCENTRIC VICTORIANA

50 **Bowery Hotel**

8 335 Bowery

Rooms from $325

There's a stuffed bulldog in the back corner of the lobby, and that only begins to indicate the eccentric and wondrous strange character of the Bowery Hotel. Another Sean MacPherson and Eric Goode creation (see also The Jane and The Park; pp. 124 and 152), the lobby of the Bowery looks like a credible recreation of a warm Victorian sitting room, with deep plush chairs, a crackling fireplace, a golden mural on the wall and a bar in the back where the Pimm's Cups flow freely. But don't be deluded: the Bowery is very au courant. Taavo Somer of nearby Freeman's (p. 137) consulted on the ground-floor Italian restaurant, Gemma, while the second-floor bar is regular host to model parties and Lindsay Lohan sightings. The 135 guestrooms also combine the old world with the new: Turkish rugs next to iPod sound docks, mohair-covered chairs next to flatscreen televisions. There's also plenty of exposed brick in the bedrooms and endless amounts of marble in the stately bathrooms. Great glass windows look out onto the East Village, beckoning you to explore, but with a large DVD collection (they've got everything from *Diva* to *Hannah and Her Sisters*) and 400 thread-count sheets, there's little incentive to leave.

## Hotel on Rivington

107 Rivington Street
Rooms from $220

This striking hotel is certainly not trying to blend in with its surroundings, as its twenty-one stories of gleaming glass soar above the 19th-century tenements that characterize the determinedly bohemian Lower East Side. Brainchild of real estate developer Paul Stallings, the hotel has attracted a lot of attention – certainly for its incongruity, but also for the bold design statement that it makes both inside and out. Young architect duo Grzywinski Pons is responsible for the tinted glass and zinc shingle exterior. The interior is a composite of the work of several prominent designers, including Marcel Wanders, who has created a sculptural entrance that resembles the curvaceous interior of an igloo, and India Mahdavi, who produced the guestroom furnishings. Each of the 110 rooms is somewhat larger than your average New York hotel room. This sense of spaciousness is only enhanced by the floor-to-ceiling windows offering views of Lower Manhattan and – on the higher floors – beyond. The rooms are designed to make the most of the urban scenery; wake-up calls, for instance, trigger motorized curtains that slide open to reveal the view. In the bathroom, the shower stall abuts the building's exterior window. Guests with less exhibitionist tendencies will be glad to hear that the designers have also installed an optional conceal-and-reveal device in the window. The bathrooms also feature decadent, oversized Japanese soaking tubs and deliciously heated Bisazza floor tiles. If you can bear to leave your tub, the second-floor lounge, facing onto the fashionable thoroughfare of Rivington Street, provides an elegant setting in which to read the papers over an espresso. Designer Pierro Lissoni is responsible for such details as the deep ebony wood and beautiful Venini chandelier.

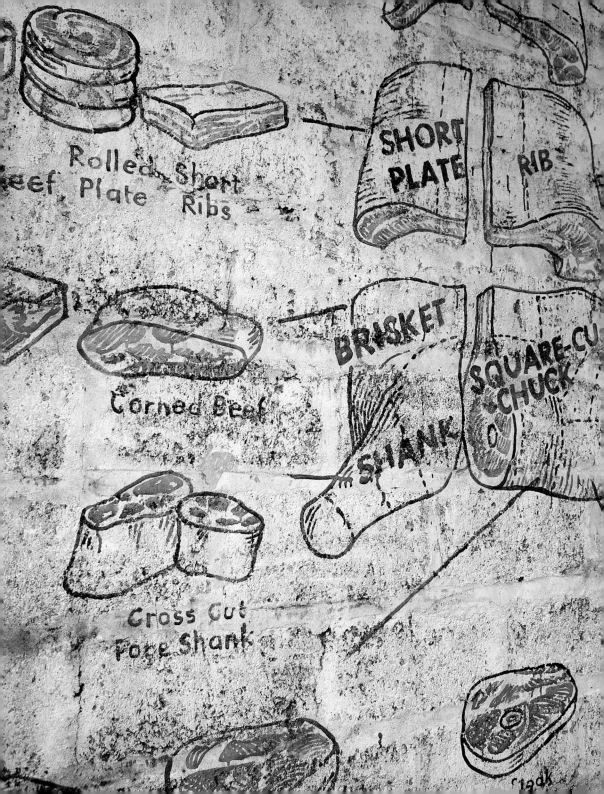

# eat

Delicious food is only one component of a successful restaurant. Those included here certainly offer a good meal, but they also manage to capture the zeitgeist of New York's dining scene. Atop the food chain is David Chang, the chef-owner of a few wildly inventive eateries, but New York is big enough to foster multiple geists at one zeit. Alongside Chang's sleek interiors runs a current of rustic Americana, fueled by the city's barbeque obsession. Eating out is a luxury, and in these unluxurious times restaurants are vanishing with dizzying speed. Nearly every one is offering a prix-fixe or "recession special" to make sweeter the bitter pill of economic woe.

# SMOKED FIS

## PRICE PER 1/4 LB

| | | |
|---|---|---|
| STURGEON | 12.00 | Whi |
| Pastrami Salmon or Gravlox | 8.75. | Whole |
| Eastern Nova Scotia Salmon | 8.75. | Center |
| Western Nova Scotia Salmon | 8.25. | Jumbo |
| elly (Salty) Lox | 6.75. | Chubs |
| ippered (Baked) Salmon | 6.75. | Raint |
| able | 8.75 | Impo |

This Jewish delicatessen, established at this location in 1927 when the Greengrass family moved their business from Harlem, provides the perfect environment in which to get a smoked-fish taste of Upper West Side life. The interior and the attitude have been cured as perfectly as their specialty sturgeon. The counters burst with three varieties of Russian caviar, smoked rainbow brook trout, pickled herrings, kippered salmon, chopped liver, pastrami and bialys. The atmosphere is that of an old diner with fluorescent lighting, and faded Formica wainscoting and vinyl are the materials of choice. Upper West Side families, writers and desiccated but immaculately turned-out old timers come here on Saturday mornings for eggs scrambled with nova and onions washed down with cream soda. You'll feel privileged to join them.

COMFORT FOOD

**50** **Freeman's**

**24** 2 Freeman Alley

Follow the stream of hungover Lower East Siders to this elusive unmarked restaurant at the end of a blind alley off Rivington Street, and tuck into a morning-after Bloody Mary and plate of eggs. Once inside, diners have the impression of having stumbled into a Highland hunting lodge. The dark walls are appointed with loops of greenery, age-spotted mirrors, old prints and stuffed ducks fastened mid-flight above the fireplace. The staff, casual with their just-out-of-bed hairdos and still-in-bed outfits, will find you a place at one of the wooden tables, set simply with candles and jam jars of wild flowers. Morning visitors are soothed by 1920s jazz music and the hiss of steaming milk. Owner and architect Taavo Somer's menu features such 1950s throwbacks as Devils on Horseback (piping-hot Stilton-stuffed prunes, wrapped in bacon), wild boar terrine with lingonberry sauce, and venison stew with kumquats and white beans. For dessert, there are stewed plums or apple Brown Betty with vanilla ice cream.

COCKTAILS
BRANDY ALEXANDE
FRENCH 75
PIMMS CUP
GIN RANDY
CHAMPAGNE COCKT
NEGRONI
BLOOD ORANGE COS
SIDECAR
BLOOD ORANGE MAR

DINER STYLE

92 **Diner**

3 85 Broadway, Brooklyn

Diner, at the epicenter of ultra-hip Williamsburg, is an uncontested mecca of cool. Ever since co-owners Andrew Tarlow and Mark Firth refurbished this battered 1927 dining car in 1999, artists and fashionistas from an ever-increasing radius have colonized its leaning banquettes on Sunday mornings or late Friday nights, to view themselves and each other nonchalantly in the bar-length strip of mirror. The music is loud – there's a DJ on weekend evenings – and the mullet-haired staff have just the right mix of friendliness and reserve. With its wobbly bar stools, cracked mosaic flooring and bunches of fresh flowers on the bar, Diner manages to retain an indefinable essence of run-down charm. The plastic-clad menu lists its good-value foods generically – "green salad," "spinach" or "burger" – in suitably basic Courier font. Wielding ballpoint pens, the waiting staff will scrawl Caroline Fidanza's specials, such as perfectly cooked whole trout or codfish hash, on your table's paper covering.

## 92 **Fette Sau**

4 354 Metropolitan Avenue, Brooklyn

Riding the barbeque wave that currently has New York in its smoky grip, Fette Sau (German for "Fat Pig") started serving moist brisket, juicy ribs and pounds of pork cheek in 2007. Kim and Joe Carroll, who own the stellar bar Spuyten Duyvil across the street, converted the former garage into an earthly temple to carnivores. There's a fresco of meat – cow, lamb and pig – on one wall, the draught-beer handles are scary looking instruments of slaughter, and Jim himself made the stools out of old tractor seats. Matt Lang, formerly of the upscale Pearl Oyster Bar, serves as pitmaster, presiding over a Southern Pride smoker that holds up to 700 pounds (318 kg) of meat and the court of hungry hipsters who crowd around the picnic benches. As befits a BBQ joint, there's a healthy selection of whiskey to wash down the ribs. When the nights are warm, the garage door rolls up and the party and cuts of pork butt (shoulder, for the uninitiated) spill out to the patio.

Megu, meaning "blessing" in Japanese, is the US debut of Japan's unstoppable restaurateur, Koji Imai. A team of twenty-five chefs presents contemporary Japanese cuisine, including *sumibi aburiyaki*, which is grilled using *binchotan*, a charcoal imported from Kyoto and prized for its purifying properties. In both Japan and the US, Imai works directly with farmers, fishermen, and local organic producers. Architect Yasumichi Morita created the spectacular two-tiered space, blending contemporary design with traditional Japanese references, such as the giant temple bell (*bonsho*) suspended from the ceiling, and the ice sculpture of a Buddha, carved each afternoon. The 205-seat dining room is overlooked by the upper-level bar, which hosts frequent sake-tasting parties. A compromise between transparency and privacy is achieved by walls of interlocking rice bowls and sake vases. White leather banquettes with soaring backs provide an intimate backdrop for such dishes as Kobe beef, grilled at the table on river stones, and foie gras teriyaki skewers.

It's 2am, you're with friends and have had a few drinks, and your mind is firmly fixed upon the idea of a burger. Your course is set for this dark and divey sports bar, where cheeseburgers and chicken sandwiches served on paper plates with all the essential condiments cost $4 and $5.50 respectively. The jukebox is well stocked with mournful music, and McSorley's ale (see p. 151) is only $2 a glass. Style and Corner Bistro are words that do not sit easily together – the clientele is regrettably of the frat boy variety – but this atmospheric corner tavern, located in the far reaches of the West Village where the street grid system breaks down most fully, is a great place to watch a game or simply nurse a bourbon on the rocks at the bar to the accompaniment of Tom Waits on the jukebox.

OYSTER VAULT

## 64  **Grand Central Oyster Bar & Restaurant**

**4**  Grand Central Station, 87 East 42nd Street

Don't be put off by the early 1980s rainbow graphics on the door; this place is timeless. Lunchtimes are best. A canny waitress will slide fresh biscuits and butter at you the minute you pick a white leatherette seat at one of the U-shaped counters and serve your food in the blink of an eye. But take your time and soak it all in, including the recently cleaned Rafael Guastavino vaulted ceilings, tiled floor and enormous paper menu of oysters, harvested from all over North America and now being shucked in big tubs at a side bar. The clientele includes few travelers, but most tourists choose the blander fast-food concessions on the food court above. Instead, the Oyster Bar is the lunchtime refuge of Midtown businessmen and quintessential New York characters who'll "take the usual, please, Jeannie," whether that's a clam chowder, an oyster pan roast, or a dozen Blue Points.

BRIGHT LIGHTS, BIG CITY

## 14  **Odeon**

**5**  145 West Broadway

The 1930s substructure of this restaurant interior is still visible after a 1980 renovation at the hands of fraternal restaurant stylists Brian and Keith McNally and owner Lynn Wagenknecht. Original fixtures such as the granite floor, the Art Deco wood paneling and pendant globe lights remain. As Jay McInerney understates in *Bright Lights, Big City*, the Odeon "makes you feel reasonable at any hour, often against bad odds." The afternoon brings daylight, severed into strips by Venetian blinds, to a Bloody Mary brunch and the small hours see a lively crew of fashionistas and artistic types crowded into red and black leather banquettes for good American bistro fare.

Le Cirque could, rightly, be called the last of the great New York restaurants. Opened in 1971 by a rakish Italian named Sirio Maccioni, Le Cirque has the *table préféré* for everyone from Robert De Niro to the Kennedy clan. The restaurant – like any forty-year-old – has gone through some changes, including moving from the Mayfair Hotel to the Palace Hotel, and now to the ground floor of the sleek Robert A. M. Stern-designed Bloomberg Center. The $18 million interior, designed by Adam Tihany, contains a classic dinner-jacket-required dining room, with a more informal bar, which is dominated by a 27-foot (8-meter) wine tower. Tihany cocoons diners in the double-story dining room under a large hanging cream "lampshade," a playful riff on a circus tent, but his design, as unbelievable as it may sound, is subtle. The real star here is the menu, which is as playful and high-flying as the decor. Craig Tompson, a young New Zealand chef, adds his own twist – like a delicious rabbit, bacon and foie gras terrine – to a menu rich with old favorites, including crème brûlée, a dish invented by Mr. Maccioni decades ago.

## 64 **Lever House Restaurant**

Have lunch and visit one of New York's most iconic corporate architectural landmarks all in one go. The steel-frame building, designed in 1952 by Gordon Bunshaft, underwent extensive renovation in 2003 and now boasts a restaurant with delectable fare prepared by executive chef Dan Silverman and pastry chef Deborah Snyder. Wanting a contemporary feel for the interior, as well as distance from the modernist structure in which it is housed, owners John McDonald (see Merc Bar; p. 25) and Josh Pickard (Joe's Pub; p. 29) commissioned designer extraordinaire Marc Newson (who also designed the Canteen restaurant in SoHo) to come up with the goods. Rising to the challenge, Newson used materials such as wood and leather to create warmth and a sense of sanctuary from the commercial hustle of Park Avenue.

## Momofuku Ssäm Bar

207 Second Avenue

David Chang, a 28-year-old former theology student, is the undisputed king of New York restaurants. His creative fusion of Japanese, Korean and Chinese cuisine – first seen at his Momofuku Noodle Bar, which opened in 2003 – blossomed into something entirely new and unusual at the Ssäm Bar. Though the original concept was as an Asian burrito bar, the place is now the late-night lab for Chang's genius. From 11 at night until 3 in the morning, diners at this sleek yet informal restaurant sit at stools or atop little ottomans to sample Chang's creations. Crispy pig's head torchon comes with aduzuki beans and cured hamachi with edamame, horseradish and pea leaves, accompanied by indie rock over the loudspeaker and served by tattooed yet friendly waitstaff. In Chang's East Village empire – which consists of the original noodle bar and the twelve-seat haute-cuisine restaurant, Ko – the Ssäm Bar is the most freewheeling, affordable and fun. Don't forget to save room for the "compost cookie" – an everything-but-the-kitchen-sink cookie by pastry wizard Christina Tosi at the adjoining Momofuku Milk Bar.

I'LL HAVE WHAT SHE'S HAVING

**50 Katz's Delicatessen**

**23** 205 East Houston Street

A stalwart institution of the Jewish Lower East Side since 1888, Katz's Delicatessen is the place to satisfy your cravings for hot pastrami and corned-beef sandwiches. Favored by presidents – even Bill Clinton's famously large appetite was apparently satiated after a sandwich (plus two more to take back to Washington) – it is also popular among actors. Meg Ryan famously demonstrated her fake orgasm in *When Harry Met Sally* at one of Katz's Formica tables. The air is thick with the smell of hanging salamis and pickles, and the bustle of regulars who handle the obstacle course necessary to obtain a sandwich with wisecracking ease.

FISH BAIT

### 14 Lure Fish Bar
**36** 142 Mercer Street

The *QEII* might dock across the river in Red Hook, but the jet-set lifestyle lives on in this cavernous subterranean SoHo restaurant. Owned by the über-stylish John McDonald (see also Merc Bar and Lever House Restaurant; pp. 25 and 143) and designed by the King Midas of New York nightlife, Serge Becker of La Esquina (p. 21) fame, Lure's cabinlike interior ingeniously weds the nautical with the culinary and exudes a mod, continental cool. You almost expect a vintage Vespa to roar in from the kitchen. Happily, the menu is drawn more from the sea than from the streets of Portofino. Eastern flavors from the raw bar, stocked with Kumamoto oysters and fluke ceviche, mix with classic favorites like clam chowder and grilled salmon with pumpkin gnocchi. During the day, Lure Fish Bar is filled with the media big fish who lunch, but at night the clientele consists of lithe SoHo models and stylish New Yorkers with an affinity for lobster rolls and cocktails.

CAFÉ CULTURE

### 14 Café Gitane
**17** 242 Mott Street

Beautiful people – lots of them – gather at Café Gitane, so expect a long line. And while the calculated insouciance of the young Italian photographer at the next table, showing contact sheets to an Austrian art director, can be a little grating, you'll forgive and forget as soon as you settle into this delightful café. With a delicate Moroccan glass of fresh mint tea in hand and a towering sandcastle of couscous to come, you can lean back amid the eddy of Nolita activity and bask in the afternoon sun streaming in across the tiled floor.

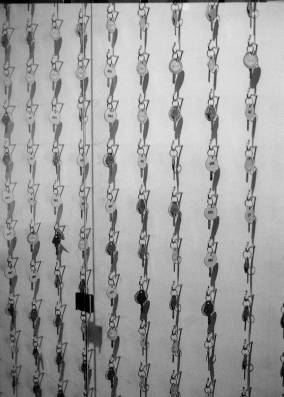

## 14 Public

28 210 Elizabeth Street

Public is the joint creation of design and concept group AvroKO, head chef Brad Farmerie, and consulting chefs Peter Gordon and Anna Hansen from London's The Providores. Their menu is bold and multicultural, combining the flavors and produce of New Zealand and Australia with Middle Eastern and Asian influences. One favorite starter is kangaroo and coriander falafel, with a lemon-tahini sauce and green pepper relish, and entrées include a concoction of monkfish cheeks, mussels and cockles, served with courgette ribbons and lemon-braised fennel. Industrial materials have been used for the interior, including concrete and rough white brick, offset by rich wooden floors and soft light emanating from the glass oil lamps converted from soap dispensers. Post office boxes lining the entryway, menus printed on pale yellow manila files and presented on clipboards, and bathroom doors with frosted glass and gold beveled numbers, salvaged from an old school, continue the utilitarian aesthetic.

# drink

New York nightlife has always been about niches. All a weary soul can ask for is a warm bar stool, a cold whiskey, and shelter from the storm. These bars offer that sense of blissful displacement, and more. The city is currently having a speakeasy moment; there are so many underground bars that one yearns for a good old above-board pub. We've included some of those – the bourbon mecca Char No. 4, for example – as well as some of the lesser known craft bars, like PDT ("Please Don't Tell") and B-Flat, in which the art of the cocktail and attention to detail are matched by the art and elegance of the surroundings.

A BEAST OF A BAR

**50** **B.East**

**32** 171 East Broadway

The best bars are often the hardest to find, and B.East, a new venue opened by architect and Santos Party House (p. 18) co-owner Ron Castellano, is worth the effort. This vegetarian restaurant is a strange and small tangle of art, alcohol and late-night dancing. The basement bar is sparse and stylish, with one wall routinely taken up with video projections. Besides beer and the other regular bar fare, B.East serves organic wine, LEED-produced champagne and a cocktail called the Zulu Basil, a concoction of TRU Organic Lemon Vodka, lemon syrup and basil sorbet.

PEOPLE-WATCHING AND COFFEE

**14** **Caffé Roma**

**14** 385 Broome Street

A thimble-full of strong espresso and a Sicilian-style cannoli from one of Little Italy's oldest pasticcerias are the perfect refreshments on a New York Saturday afternoon. Sit at a marble-topped table near the window and watch the bustle go by. Relics of late 19th-century Little Italy, such as the pressed-tin ceiling, a saloon clock that hangs over the espresso machine, and the wood-backed bar behind the takeaway pastry counter, remain undisturbed thanks to the longtime family running of the business.

"There is a thick musty smell that acts as a balm to jerky nerves; it is really a rich compound of the smells of pine sawdust, tap drippings, pipe tobacco, coal smoke, and onions." So wrote Joseph Mitchell in his 1942 book *McSorley's Wonderful Saloon.* These days the best time to visit this venerable institution is the afternoon, when shafts of sunlight slice through the dense atmosphere and you can banter with the Irish barkeeps. First opened in 1854, it took 116 years for McSorley's to allow women across the threshold.

Nightlife impresarios Sean MacPherson and Eric Goode (the duo behind The Jane and Bowery hotels; pp. 124 and 130) hired design guru Jim Walrod to conceive their latest restaurant and lounge. They took three taxi garages and turned them into an enormous theme park whose interior references country lodge and opium den in equal measure. A Dracaena tree, gold-dipped Mies van der Rohe Barcelona chairs, giant benches cut from tree trunks, and crackling fires all add their own notes and contribute to a rare oasis in an industrial West Chelsea setting.

**104** **Sherwood Café at Robin des Bois**

**8** 195 Smith Street, Brooklyn

After outfitting many of Manhattan's better known French bistros, Bernard Decanali opened a café of his own in his Boerum Hill antiques shop. In the summer the leafy garden, with its eclectic assortment of seating and old enamel advertising signage, is a great place for a few bottles of wine and fantastic snacking fare. Inside, the crazy collection of objects – such as stuffed crocodiles, 1950s hatstands and chandeliers, stacked Parisian salon-style from floor to ceiling – combines with a clientele that easily mixes families and local hipsters.

```
—  F O O D    M E N U  —

PICKLED  EGG              1
PICKLE                    2
OYSTER                    3
PRETZEL  DOG              4
ICEBERG  WEDGE            7
HERB  POTATO  WEDGES      8
TURKEY  PILGRIM          11
PULLED  PORK  SANDWICH   11
MINI FISH  PO  BOYS      12
WARM  COOKIES             3

HAPPY HOUR M▶—▶F 5PM TO 7PM
    KITCHEN  OPEN  6PM TO 2 AM

18% DRUNK TAX ADDED TO  ANY
   ABANDONED  CREDIT CARDS
   LOW  TIDE        HIGH TIDE
   554 AM          1:38 PM
   SUNRISE          SUN SE
   535 AM           5 58PM
```

32  MEAT LOAF IN MARGARITAVILLE

**23**
## The Rusty Knot
425 West Street

For their newest bar, Taavo Somer and Ken Friedman
have channeled an alternative Jimmy Buffet universe. It
may seem contrived, yet as the sun filters through the slat
blinds, the jukebox plays "Barracuda" by Heart and the
crack of pool balls fills the room, you can't help but feel
your cynicism slowly evaporate. This may be the result of
the very strong rum cocktails, or perhaps the vertiginously
hip crowd. The menu, designed by ex-Momofuker
(p. 144) Joaquin Baca, includes a stellar meat loaf
sandwich. Not quite a cheeseburger in paradise, but close.

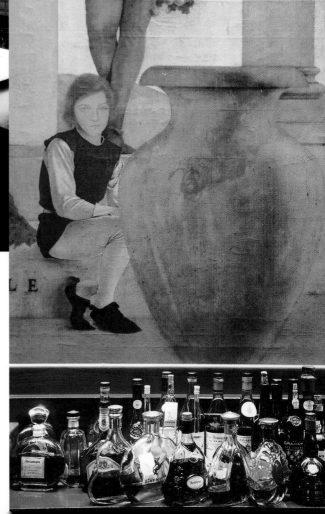

MIDTOWN MERRIMENT
## 64 King Cole Bar
**13** St. Regis Hotel, 2 East 55th Street

Legend has it that this dark and magical bar tucked off the lobby of the swanky St. Regis hotel is the birthplace of the Bloody Mary, which here goes by its original name, the Red Snapper. After a couple of these potent, spicy concoctions, accompanied by liberal servings of salted almonds and macadamia nuts, you will feel that you are, like the eponymous nursery rhyme hero of the bar's spectacular Maxfield Parrish mural, a "merry old soul." The wood-paneled warmth and the deep banquettes provide blissful refuge from the crowds of Fifth Avenue.

PLEASE DON'T TELL
## 50 PDT
**17** 113 St. Mark's Place

Behind Crif Dogs is the entrance to PDT, a bar that oozes charm and offers cocktails made by top mixologist Jim Meehan, along with lush leather booths and the occasional taxidermied creature. There's a soft, classy glow about the place that only grows softer with each Paddington, a combination of white rum, citrus, lillet, absinthe and orange marmalade. For hungry tipplers, Crif hot dogs, including the Wylie Dog, topped with deep-fried mayo and dried onions by Wylie Dufresne of WD-50 (p. 58), is passed through a small hole in the wall.

## 14 29 B-Flat Bar

B-Flat Bar, a windowless subterranean room in Tribeca, is serious about being cool. The vibe is grown-up and sophisticated, a tonic to the city's scenester hotspots. The dark wood bar, the Japanese bartenders in matching maroon vests and armbands, the soft lighting and live jazz form a cocoon of Godardian cool. Belmondo wouldn't feel out of place in one of the booths. Giant Steps (a cocktail named for the John Coltrane song) is a brisk and well-balanced wasabi-infused vodka and sake combination that captures B-Flat's mix of Eastern and Western cultures.

CLANDESTINE COCKT
## 50 14 Angel's Share
8 Stuyvesant Street

It is a combination of strict house rules – no standing, no groups of more than four, no shouting – and an out-of-the-way location at the rear of a second-floor fluorescent-lit Japanese restaurant that helps screen the crowds at this jewel of a bar. For even more privacy, seek out the curtained-off section at the end of the narrow space. The old-school cocktails are mixed with cool precision by some of the most skilled bartenders in town. Named for the portion of alcohol that's lost to the "angels" during the aging process, this bar breathes nothing but refinement.

## Bohemian Hall & Beer Garden
29–19 24th Avenue, Queens

The Bohemian Hall & Beer Garden was built in 1910 by the Bohemian Citizens' Benevolent Society for Astoria's transplanted population of Czechs. Members of this fraternal society who had day jobs as masons, plumbers and electricians volunteered their services to construct the hall, and transformed a patch of Long Island farmland into an authentic European beer garden. At one time there were more than 800 such beer gardens in New York, but today this is the only that one survives. Spend a leisurely summer evening in this garden that with its picnic tables, bandstand, and trees hung with bunting has the feel of an Eastern European village square. The drink of choice here is Pilsner Urqell by the pint, and barbeque stations cater to your kielbasa and sauerkraut cravings. You may even end up dancing to the strident tunes of a Slovak folk band.

WHISKEY PALACE

104
5

## Char No. 4
196 Smith Street, Brooklyn

Bourbon, a whiskey made with corn in the bluegrass hills of Kentucky, has somewhat strangely found purchase on this bar-and-resto studded stretch of Smith Street. At Char No. 4, watched over by hundreds of whiskey bottles and large barrel-shaped lights, a young Cobble Hill crowd tipples on "every whiskey known to man," according Sean Josephs, one of the owners. That's a lot of whiskey. The bar opened in 2008 when Michael Tsoumpas, a whiskey fanatic, decided to do something about the 400-plus bottles he had amassed. Many of them made their way onto the shelf – the very, very top shelf – including a discontinued Maker's Mark Black Wax Black Label that goes for $100 an ounce. There are also cheaper whiskeys and cocktails like the Nor'Easter ("a bourbon, dark and stormy"). Although the owners are serious about whiskey – 'char no. 4' is the degree of smokiness of whiskey barrels – there's some good grub to be had here, too. The chef, Texan-born Matt Greco, combines his haute-cuisine background with his backwoods upbringing on dishes like shrimp and grits and a biscuit eggs Benedict.

## 14 Apotheke
### 9 9 Doyers Street

Tucked into an obscure elbow of Chinatown's Doyers Street, Apotheke is part alchemist den, part speakeasy. Once inside the unmarked door, you'll find Viennese mixologist Albert Trummer behind the custom-made bar, surrounded by beakers and graduated cylinders. His "elixirs" include the ever-popular Cilantro Passo – cilantro-infused gin, muddled cucumber, agave nectar and fresh lime. The space, says owner Helen Tierney, was inspired by "ancient apothecaries in Europe, absinthe dens in Paris during the Belle Époque, and the seediness of Chinatown."

CHURCH OF VODKA
14 **Temple Bar**
332 Lafayette Street

Like some strange clue in an Indiana Jones movie, the
silhouette of an iguana skeleton on the wall at 332 Lafayette
Street is the Temple Bar's only marker. Inside, the plush
dark interior, magnificent cherry-oak bar, black marble
and dim Art Deco sconces are seductively enveloping.
Try one of a massive collection of vodkas with a bowl
of spicy popcorn, or choose from a bar menu that includes
fresh oysters on the half shell, Beluga caviar, salmon
canapés and Angus steak skewers. Then try to leave.
You'll find that time has its own measure in this alcohol-
hazed shrine.

# shop

When it comes to shopping, New York has an unrivaled gravitational pull. Designers and discerning shoppers from around the world flock to the city, where the market for the avant-garde, the experimental and the sartorially intellectual is ever hungry. There is an abundance of outlets for their work from high-end emporia like Bergdorf Goodman on Fifth Avenue to carefully curated micro-boutiques in Nolita. The array is dizzying. Store owners are the unsung heroes of capitalism, with these stellar destinations in particular offering well-chosen goods in well-appointed settings. Good for buying, and even better for browsing.

STYLE IMMERSION

78 **Barneys**

2 660 Madison Avenue

At this axis of New York style (with the most decadent of Christmas window displays in town), you'll indulge in a truly luxurious shopping experience that spans nine floors displaying thousands of products and ends with lunch and top-quality people-watching at Fred's restaurant on the basement level. Minimalist architect Peter Marino was commissioned in 1993 by the Pressman family to convert the 1955 building at Madison Avenue and 61st Street into the 230,000 square feet (21,350 square meters) of unmissable New York event that Barneys is today.

UPTOWN BARGAINS DOWNTOWN

32 **Barneys Co-op**

10 236 West 18th Street

The downtown branches of the uptown department store carry such labels as Daryl K, Katayone Adeli, Jill Stuart and Vivienne Tam, less expensive and more street-inspired than those stocked by their uptown big sister. If you are in the city in August or February, you are in for the fashion spectacle of the Barney's Warehouse Sale, when the Chelsea store slashes prices up to 80 percent. Watch out for the stampede of well-heeled women trying to get to that sexy-secretary Marc Jacobs cashmere cardigan. The SoHo branch is located at 116 Wooster Street.

Subterranean boutique I Heart stocks a superb range of girlie clothing from such happening labels as Mary Ping's Slow and Steady Wins the Race and Surface to Air, along with fashionable housewares, like David Wiseman's ceramic hat hangers in the shape of deer heads, and books from the cultish Die Gestalten Verlag. Owners Antonia Kojuharova and Jill Bradshaw also curate a series of exhibitions by graphic artists for those less inclined to part with their cash.

Kari Sigerson's and Miranda Morrison's line of mint-green lined shoes have been a hit with the ladies who lunch ever since they opened their small store in Nolita eight years ago. The newer, larger location, once a vegetable warehouse, features a storefront grid of aluminum, glass and white "penny tile," which affords enticing views of the luminous interior. Inside, movable brushed-steel tables display their signature kitten-heeled mules and buckled Mary Janes, and a long red banquette designed for Cappellini by Miranda's brother, Jasper.

Knives, pendants and rings carefully draped over driftwood set inside antique display cases fill at least half of this eponymous boutique. The other half is a tiny workshop where Hannah Clark, as much curator as creator, crafts custom wedding rings. A small knife made of a bobcat's jaw is the work of Peddler, a "Catskills mountain man," while the Egyptian-style hammered necklaces on the wall are by Lou Zeldis, a Balinese-based artist. Clark's own work, including a gold pendant featuring the words "Take it easy, but take it," combines Woody Guthrie's anti-establishment sentiment with beautiful craftsmanship.

Beth Buccini and Sarah Easley are the minds behind this fascinatingly eclectic SoHo store, which they tout as a "saccharine-free supermarket of style." In 1999 they commissioned Nick Dine to design the rainbow interior, which includes a lavender resin floor, pink uplights and cornflower-blue neoprene seats. With racks loaded with desirable pieces by such designers such as Bruce, Martine Sitbon and Matthew Williamson, this original boutique has garnered a devoted fashion following. There is even a range of designer pet paraphernalia downstairs.

Ironically, one of the most innovative stores in New York started out as a side project for side projects. In 2003, Brian Janusiak and his wife Elizabeth Beer formed the design studio, Various Projects. "We had all these projects," says Janusiak, "but we were interested in concepts surrounding distribution." Janusiak and Beer, who also runs a gallery in Berlin, started keeping track of the "meanderings and explorations" of the talented coterie of artists and friends they met in New York and at art fairs around the world. The result: a light, sparse store in a former mahjong/massage parlour in Chinatown filled with strange and wondrous finds. Metalworker Chris Bundy's line of springbok horn and hippo tooth jewelry sits next to a previous Various Projects project, a brick wrapped in angora. In addition to showing little known New York designers, Project No. 8 also curates international avant-gardists, including Kostas Murkudis (Berlin), Boudicca (London) and Natalia Brilli (Paris).

Seattlite David Alhadeff opened Future Perfect in Williamsburg to showcase accessories, home furnishings and artwork by up-and-coming designers, many of them from Brooklyn. Much of the work embraces themes of irony and nostalgia, along with a contemporary reinvestigation of decoration. There are several ornamental wallpapers to choose from, and Tobias Wong's "I F*ck for Gucci" limited-edition print is typical of the store's cutting-edge inventory, as is Jason Miller's ceramic Superordinate Antler table lamp. Another thematic undercurrent of the store is sustainability, and many of the products make use of recycled materials. A line of dishware, titled 50¢, is made from vintage dishes that have been reglazed with new patterns, and the Stop It lounge chair is made from black and white rubber stoppers.

When partners Renata Bokalo and Roman Luba opened their pitch-perfect designer lifestyle store in 1999, they also pioneered a retail revolution in the Meatpacking District. The area is now New York's design and fashion Grand Central – much to the bemusement of the few remaining meat packers still operating in the area. Auto features the work of Brooklyn-based designers who manage to combine craftsmanship and knowing modernity in their household objects and accessories: leather flowers by Red Head Amy, stitched pillows by Judy Ross, and much, much more.

Former fashion entrepreneur Murray Moss's white-cube, industrial-design store in SoHo blurs the distinction between museum and shop. The covetable porcelain tableware, crystal and cutlery are presented in thematic association with one another, and contextualized with furniture and lighting. One may find a Hella Jongerius ceramic pot next to a stainless-steel Fisher space pen, next to an Edra pink leather Flap sofa. An adjacent gallery provides in-depth looks at the work of such designer/artists as Tord Boontje and the Campanor Brothers.

**Bond 07**

7 Bond Street

Tunisian-born Selima Salaun has a veritable empire of New York stores featuring her signature quirky sensibility and range of acid-bright eyeglasses. The latest is a gem of a boutique at 25 Prince Street called Lunettes et Chocolat, which takes niche retailing to a delightful extreme by selling only eyeglasses and delicious handmade chocolates. Another of her creations is Le Corset Boutique at 80 Thompson Street, which specializes in gorgeously over-the-top lingerie and loungewear. Bond 07, yet another of her coterie, is situated on NoHo's hip Bond Street (Daryl K and Ghost are among the storefronts that punctuate the brick and marble-trimmed row houses and quirky residential lofts). This one-stop shop for stylists focuses on a handpicked selection of accessories, such as hats and vintage Cartier, Rolex and Gucci watches.

Michele Quan and Robin Renzi are jewelry designers who draw their collective inspiration from nature and Middle Eastern themes to make stackable rings, necklaces, bracelets and anklets in silver and gold, using both semiprecious and rare stones and often featuring symbolic carving. This Elizabeth Street store was designed by the New York-based vanguard architectural firm, SHoP. Minimal in design, its one fanfare is a cast-in-place cement basin in the window filled with water and floating flowers.

This emporium of high-end cosmetics and hair and skincare products – the formulae for which have been passed down through the generations since the store opened as an apothecary in 1851 – is an integral part of New York's heritage. White-lab-coated staff ply you with samples and, using the same plain speaking as the products' no-frills packaging, answer your every beauty-related query. The setting is bizarre: half of the shop houses a collection of vintage motorcycles set on a floral rug before a wall of photographs of customers' babies.

**14** **Prada**
**45** 575 Broadway

Rem Koolhaas's retail laboratory for Prada arrived in a flurry of media attention in 2001. Its position at the hub of SoHo and the fact that it runs a whole block means that you can hardly miss it. Its imagination-catching interior features include the "wave," a concave shape lined with polished zebra wood that runs the length and height of the store; a glass elevator that displays merchandise; and a baroquely wallpapered north wall created by graphic designers, 2x4. Groundbreaking technological gadgets abound in this "museum show on indefinite display."

IT'S A MAN'S WORLD
**14** **Jack Spade**
**33** 56 Greene Street

Jack Spade's signature all-terrain canvas and waxwear bags, jackets and notebooks are presented back-to-back with vintage props such as Braun turntables, *Playboy* magazines, globes and balsa-wood airplanes in this 500-square-foot (46-square-meter) SoHo space designed by Stephen Sclaroff. The well-curated collection is the work of Andy Spade (Kate's husband; see her many boutiques throughout the city and her handbags on every young Manhattanite's arm) and might well stand as New York's riposte to UK über-designer Paul Smith.

## 14 | **Seize sur Vingt**
**21** 243 Elizabeth Street

This loft-style Nolita store contains a few rolling racks of clean, beautifully cut men's and women's Egyptian cotton button-down shirts and a magnificent Tascam thirty-two reel-to-reel tape recorder. The back third of the store is devoted to the shop's first-rate made-to-measure business. The look of the suits, jackets, trousers and shirts is modern and clean, but husband-and-wife team James and Gwendolyn Jurney use old-world tailoring techniques, such as single-needle stitching for the shirts, and the suits are mostly handsewn.

32 **Marc Jacobs**

35 • 385 Bleecker Street (accessories & shoes)
• 403–5 Bleecker Street (Marc by Marc Jacobs)

Despite his international success and residence in Paris, Marc Jacobs – who trained at New York's Parsons School of Design – truly belongs to this city. Barneys' (p. 162) painted advertising hoardings once declared "We Love Marc Jacobs," and Manhattan's best-dressed people show no signs of letting their devotion dwindle. These outpost stores were designed by Stephen Jaklitsch and are nestled on the most gorgeous two-block stretch of Bleecker Street (between Bank and Perry Streets) alongside Magnolia

Bakery (p. 45), Lulu Guinness and a flower shop with beautiful window displays. The company's popular secondary line, Marc by Marc Jacobs, features accessories such as his signature chunky latched and zippered handbags and round-toed, Minnie Mouse-style pumps and flats. Another store, featuring his ready-to-wear and men's collections, is located in SoHo (163 Mercer Street).

 **Mayle**

**20** 252 Elizabeth Street

In an exquisitely assembled boutique in the heart of Nolita, Brit designer and ex-model Jane Mayle and her gorgeous assistants sell lace dresses and fluttery silk floral blouses that you can pair with librarian-chic leather-edged tweed skirts. Among the racks of this sweet-smelling store – Mayle was responsible for initiating the craze for Votivo red-currant candles – are showcased accessories and other objets d'art such as a Julian Schnabel exhibition poster from 1989. Mayle says her work is inspired by the style of 1950s Italian film star Monica Vitti, whose wardrobe defined feminine elegance. Courtney Love and Sofia Coppola are among the fans of Mayle's off-the-shoulder chemises and crocheted shawls.

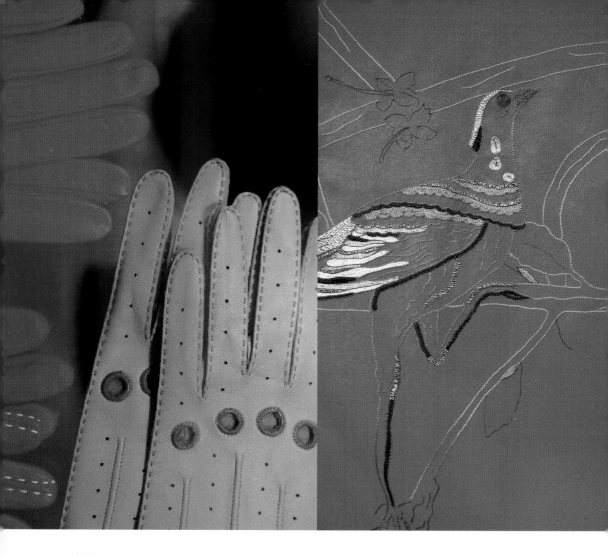

MYTHICAL MERCHANDISE

32 **Castor & Pollux**

41 238 West 10th Street

Co-owners Anne-Catherine Lüke and Kerrilynn Hunt are the ladies with the shared vision behind this intimate boutique. Their combined interior design and fashion expertise infuses both the visual character of the store – which they composed themselves from customized fixtures and antiques – and the carefully honed trove of whimsical accessories and clothing that it stows. Clutch wallets by Abas, jewelry by Melissa Joy Manning, and a range of classic underwear by On Gossamer are juxtaposed with the kinds of objects that, as they put it, "you would find in one of our apartments." Lüke and Hunt design their own signature line that puts ladylike chic in an urban context. Their store, tucked into a quiet West Village side street, carries out the lines' ethos. Vintage cases from Bergdorf Goodman's fur department, luxurious carpeting and horses, Kerrilynn's favorite animal, form a chic and quiet retail cocoon.

DESIGN FOR SALE

 **64** **MoMA Design and Book Store**

**6** 11 West 53rd Street

After a trundle round the Museum of Modern Art and its fabulous bar (p. 67), you'll also appreciate Richard Gluckman's retail spaces found throughout the museum. On the first floor, MoMA Design and Book Store features books, art reproductions and design objects, and an exhibition shop on the sixth floor showcases products related to temporary exhibitions, further blurring the distinction between museum and retail experience.

STREET-STYLE GENERAL STORE

**14** **Steven Alan**

**1** 103 Franklin Street

This Tribeca emporium of emerging designers was conceived as an old-fashioned general store, with rolling ladders that slide along ceiling-high wooden shelves stacked with La Cosa T-shirts and a 1940s pharmacy display case containing Dr. Hauschka cosmetic products. Labels are from the likes of APC, Wink, Martin Margiela 6 and Katayone Adeli. An upholstered bench is flanked by two listening stations whose sample sounds are changed bi-weekly by the people at Other Music (p. 29).

# retreat

New Yorkers know that weekend-long releases from the pressure of the city are essential for their long-term survival. Luckily for the time-deficient — visitors and residents alike — a mere 100-mile (160-kilometer) radius of Manhattan encompasses a topographical variety with ample potential for both active and contemplative diversion: from the seaside shenanigans of the Hamptons to the high-altitude hippie hangouts of the Catskill Mountains, the history-rich rolling pastures of Pennsylvania's Bucks County to the art-world destination found in the deep wooded valley carved by the Hudson River.

## Catskills: A Countercultural Escape

- Storm King Art Center
- Café Tamayo
- The Villa at Saugerties

The Catskill Mountains is a spectacular wilderness, which, with Woodstock as its unofficial capital, is the counterculture's retreat of choice. The area has also caught the attention of those New Yorkers who have been priced out of the Hamptons and are now casting about for an alternative Arcadia. To join them, from Manhattan, take the George Washington Bridge to the Palisades Parkway North for a scenic drive up the west bank of the Hudson River. Make a stop at Storm King Art Center, a magnificent sculpture park that ranges over 500 acres (200 hectares) of landscaped lawns, fields, and woodlands ornamented by monumental pieces by postwar American and European artists such as Alexander Calder, David Smith and Andy Goldsworthy, whose stone wall, winding in and out of the trees, is worth the trip alone.

Further into the Catskills is the small town of Saugerties, the site of the second 1960s Woodstock rock festival and home to those quintessential American main streets. Yes, there are antiques shops, but they are interspersed with a bay-windowed candy shop, a hardware store with its brightly colored wheelbarrows upended on the sidewalk, and an old-fashioned cinema. The small selection of restaurants includes a great place called Café Tamayo, offering New American bistro fare in an interior decorated with 19th-century paddle fans.

The Villa at Saugerties is a contemporary bed and breakfast in a 1929 Spanish-style villa with an ochre stucco exterior and red tile roof, set in a pastoral setting down a back road outside the town. Owners Aimee Szparaga and Richard Nocera are young Manhattanites who upped sticks to set up a "modern country escape." With its palette of gray and magenta, the living area has modern Danish pieces and features an exposed bluestone fireplace. Details such as bunches of fresh flowers, throw cushions by Jonathan Adler, and copies of *Visionaire* magazine ease discerning urbanites into their country refuge. In clement weather, guests can eat breakfast underneath a spreading sycamore tree on the patio outside, near the pristine swimming pool.

## Bucks County: Eccentricity and Antiques
- Fonthill
- Mercer Museum
- Golden Nugget Antique Flea Market
- Lambertville Antique Flea Market

The bucolic meadows, covered bridges and stone farmhouses of Bucks County in eastern Pennsylvania have long held artists, writers and weekenders in their thrall. In the 1930s and 1940s, New York's literati made the towns dotted along the Delaware River the scene of their voluntary exile. Dorothy Parker, the acerbic wit of the Algonquin Round Table (see p. 72), gravitated to a fourteen-room manse in Piperville, and lyricist Oscar Hammerstein resettled on a farm in Doylestown. Today, while the town of New Hope has become rather touristy, there is still plenty for those drawn to antiques and history with a bit of whimsy, or just beautiful countryside.

Archaeologist, architect, fiddler, tilemaker and erudite collector, Henry Chapman Mercer left his mark firmly upon Doylestown, where he spent all of his life. Mercer's dream house – a demented sandcastle of a mansion named Fonthill – which he built by hand between 1908 and 1912, is made from hand-poured reinforced concrete. As a leading figure of the Arts and Crafts movement, Mercer established a tilemaking factory and Fonthill is lined with his handmade colorful, often narrative-depicting tiles. The Mercer Museum holds his collection of more than 50,000 tools of early American crafts and trades and everyday household objects used in America from 1700 to 1850. To add to your own collection of Americana, cross the river to Lambertville, an unpretentious town with a colonial-village feel and the site of the famous Lambertville Golden Nugget flea markets, both on River Road.

## Hudson River Valley: Ancient Landscape, Contemporary Art

- Dia:Beacon
- Pig Hill Inn
- East Side Kitchen

Beacon is a small 18th- and 19th-century town on the banks of the Hudson River, 60 miles (100 kilometers) and so many fashion cycles north of Manhattan. And yet this sleepy town is home to the Dia Art Foundation's permanent collection of major works of art from the 1960s to the present, and thus a hot spot on the international map of contemporary art. The museum – collaboratively planned by Robert Irwin and project architect OpenOffice – occupies a 1929 steel, concrete and glass printing factory on the Hudson. The gritty industrial town itself is of interest, too. A burgeoning art scene has brought artists and galleries to the warehouse buildings, and dozens of excellent antiques shops flank the main street.

Beacon's riches do not, as yet, include any accommodations, so it is advisable to use as a base the quaint village of Cold Spring, some 10 miles (16 kilometers) to the south. Here, too, is a pleasing collection of antiques shops, bookstores and tearooms lining the main street under ornate cornices. But the real treat lies at the end of the street, where it meets the Hudson River. The views – of the stretch upstream and down, where the river narrows and deepens, and of the opposite bank, formed of primeval-looking masses of granite and dense green forest – are spectacular. Artists of the Hudson River School, such as Thomas Cole and Asher B. Durand, were similarly fascinated by this tract through the Appalachian Mountain range.

The Pig Hill Inn is the place to stay. Housed in an 1820 brick building on the main street, the inn has nine guestrooms, each appointed with antiques that are for sale, and most have wood stoves. Breakfast can be taken in your four-poster bed, in the dining room, or in the quiet garden out back. If you need a snack during the day, simply cross the street to the East Side Kitchen for a milkshake or burger in the playfully retro diner given a makeover by a couple of East Village musicians.

Long Island's eastern beaches are gorgeous broad swathes of pale sand, backed with low picket fences and dune grasses. Between the months of May and September, however, they are littered with high-strung New Yorkers "getting away from it all." Enormous ersatz mansions replete with back-garden polo fields for the likes of Sean "P. Diddy" Combs and Steven Spielberg have replaced the once-flat open potato fields that unfolded to the Atlantic. And yet, the clear light, the charm of such villages as Amagansett and the exhilarating sense of escape at Montauk, the South Fork's tip, ensure that the Hamptons remain a lovely retreat, particularly during September. East Hampton, with its boutiques and specialty shops, is easily accessible by bus or train and provides a good base. Just to the north, in a rural hamlet called The Springs, is the cottage and studio where Jackson Pollock created his most important works between 1946 and his death ten years later. The house has been left beautifully intact so that you can still browse through the artist's library and large collection of jazz records, and see the paint splatters on the floor. Bridgehampton, the next town to the west of East Hampton, is home to the Dan Flavin Art Institute, a permanent installation of nine of Flavin's works in fluorescent light in a renovated firehouse building.

Most New Yorkers rent houses in the summer, and for short stays there are only a handful of interesting lodgings. One such place is Andre Balazs's twenty-room Sunset Beach Hotel on Shelter Island, situated between the North and South Forks of Long Island. Another option is the 1770 House on East Hampton's Main Street, within easy reach of the boutiques and the secluded Egypt beach. Designer Laura Maerov, who recently restored the inn, has combined traditional wallpapers, wood paneling and eclectic antiques to give each room individual charm. The destination restaurant serves seasonal American cuisine by local star chef, Kevin Penner.

# contact

All telephone numbers are given for dialling locally, but a '1' must be dialled before the ten-digit number when calling from outside the area code (i.e., 212 or 718). From abroad, the country code is +1, followed by the ten-digit number, without an additional '1'. The same applies for telephone numbers in the retreat section. The number in brackets by the name is the page number on which the entry appears.

**A Bathing Ape** [22]
91 Greene Street
New York, NY 10012
T   212 925 0222
W   www.bape.com

**Abyssinian Baptist Church** [88]
132 Odell Clark Place
New York, NY 10030
T   212 862 7474
E   info@abyssinian.org
W   www.abyssinian.org

**Albanese Meats & Poultry** [18]
238 Elizabeth Street
New York, NY 10012
T   212 966 1788

**Alessi** [25]
130 Greene Street
New York, NY 10012
T   212 941 7300
E   retail.soho@alessi.com
W   www.alessi.com

**Algonquin Hotel** [72]
59 West 44th Street
New York, NY 10036
T   212 840 6800
W   www.thealgonquin.net

**Alias Café** [58]
76 Clinton Street
New York, NY 10002

T   212 505 5011
W   www.aliasrestaurant.com

**Alpana Bawa** [56]
70 East 1st Street
New York, NY 10003
T   212 254 1249
E   alpana@alpanabawa.com
W   www.alpanabawa.com

**American Folk Art Museum** [73]
45 West 53rd Street
New York, NY 10019
T   212 265 1040
E   info@folkartmuseum.org
W   www.folkartmuseum.org

**Angel Orensanz Foundation** [58]
172 Norfolk Street
New York, NY 10002
T   212 529 7194
E   info@orensanz.org
W   www.orensanz.org

**Angel's Share** [156]
8 Stuyvesant Street
New York, NY 10003
T   212 777 5415

**Annex Antiques Fair and Flea Market** [36]
Sixth Avenue, between
24th and 26th Streets
New York, NY 10003

T   212 243 5343
E   info@
    hellskitchenfleamarket.com
W   www.
    hellskitchenfleamarket.com

**Another Room** [17]
249 West Broadway
New York, NY 10013
T   212 226 1418
W   www.theotheroom.com

**Apotheke** [158]
9 Doyers Street
New York, NY 10013
T   212 406 0400
E   info@apothekebar.com
W   www.apothekebar.com

**Apple Store** [26]
103 Prince Street
New York, NY 10012
T   212 226 3126
W   www.apple.com/retail/soho

**Artists Space** [22]
38 Greene Street, 3rd Floor
New York, NY 10013
T   212 226 3970
E   info@artistsspace.org
W   www.artistsspace.org

**Asia Society** [81]
725 Park Avenue
New York, NY 10021
T   212 288 6400

E   info@asiasociety.org
W   www.asiasociety.org

**Auto** [167]
805 Washington Street
New York, NY 10014
T   212 229 2292
E   shop@thisisauto.com
W   www.thisisauto.com

**Balthazar** [22]
80 Spring Street
New York, NY 10012
T   212 965 1414
W   www.balthazarny.com

**Bar Room at the Modern** [67]
Museum of Modern Art
9 West 53rd Street
New York, NY 10019
T   212 333 1220
E   info@themodernnyc.com
W   www.themodernnyc.com

**Barney Greengrass** [136]
541 Amsterdam Avenue
New York, NY 10024
T   212 724 4707
E   info@barneygreengrass.com
W   www.barneygreengrass.com

**Barneys** [162]
660 Madison Avenue
New York, NY 10065
T   212 826 8900

E info-madison@barneys.com
W www.barneys.com

**Barneys Co-op** [162]
236 West 18th Street
New York, NY 10011
116 Wooster Street
New York, NY 10012
T 212 593 7800
E info-coop18@barneys.com
W www.barneys.com

**Bayard Building** [29]
65 Bleecker Street
New York, NY 10012

**B.East** [150]
171 East Broadway
New York, NY 10002
T 212 228 3100
E beast@broadwayeast.com
W www.broadwayeast.com

**Bed and Breakfast on
the Park** [114]
113 Prospect Park West
Brooklyn, NY 11215
T 718 499 6115
E contact@bbnyc.com
W www.bbnyc.com

**Bemelmans Bar** [82]
Carlyle Hotel
35 East 76th Street
New York, NY 10021
T 212 744 1600
E thecarlyle@
rosewoodhotels.com
W www.thecarlyle.com

**B-Flat Bar** [156]
277 Church Street
New York, NY 10013
T 212 219 2970
W www.bflat.info

**Bid Brasserie** [81]
1334 York Avenue
New York, NY 10021
T 212 988 7730

**Bohemian Hall & Beer
Garden** [157]
29–19 24th Avenue
Astoria, NY 11102
T 718 274 4925
E manager@bohemianhall.com
W www.bohemianhall.com

**Bond 07** [168]
7 Bond Street
New York, NY 10012
T 212 677 8487
W www.selimaoptique.com

**Bond No. 9** [29]
9 Bond Street
New York, NY 10012
T 212 228 1732
E contactus@bondno9.com
W www.bondno9.com

**Bottino** [38]
246 Tenth Avenue
New York, NY 10001
T 212 206 6766
E info@bottinonyc.com
W www.bottinonyc.com

**Bouley** [16]
163 Duane Street
New York, NY 10013
T 212 964 2525
E info@bouleynyc.com
W www.davidbouley.com

**Bowery Hotel** [130]
335 Bowery
New York, NY 10003
T 212 505 9100
E info@bohonyc.com
W www.theboweryhotel.com

**Brasserie** [71]
Seagram Building
100 East 53rd Street
New York, NY 10022
T 212 751 4840
W www.patinagroup.com/
east/brasserie

**Bridge Café** [60]
279 Water Street
New York, NY 10038
T 212 227 3344
E bridgecafenyc@aol.com

**Brooklyn Academy
of Music** [109]
30 Lafayette Avenue
Brooklyn, NY 11217
T 718 636 4100
E info@bam.org
W www.bam.org

**Brooklyn Botanic
Garden** [106]
1000 Washington Avenue
Brooklyn, NY 11225
T 718 623 7200
W www.bbg.org

**Brooklyn Inn** [106]
148 Hoyt Street
Brooklyn, NY 11217
T 718 625 9741

**Brooklyn Museum** [106]
200 Eastern Parkway
Brooklyn, NY 11238
T 718 638 5000
E information@
brooklynmuseum.org
W www.brooklynmuseum.org

**Brooklyn Superhero
Supply Co.** [106]
372 Fifth Avenue
Brooklyn, NY 11215
T 718 499 9884
W www.superherosupplies.com

**Brown Café + Orange** [60]
61 Hester Street
New York, NY 10002

T 212 477 2427 (Brown Café)
T 212 254 9825 (Orange)
W www.greenbrownorange.com

**Built By Wendy** [95]
46 North 6th Street
Brooklyn, NY 11002
T 718 384 2882
E info@builtbywendy.com
W www.builtbywendy.com

**Café des Artistes** [86]
1 West 67th Street
New York, NY 10023
T 212 877 3500
E info@cafenyc.com
W www.cafenyc.com

**Café Gitane** [146]
242 Mott Street
New York, NY 10012
T 212 334 9552

**Café Habana** [21]
17 Prince Street
New York, NY 10012
T 212 625 2002

**Café Luxembourg** [86]
200 West 70th Street
New York, NY 10023
T 212 873 7411
W www.cafeluxembourg.com

**Café Sabarsky** [85]
Neue Galerie
1048 Fifth Avenue
New York, NY, 10028
T 212 288 0665
W www.cafesabarsky.com

**Caffè Roma** [150]
385 Broome Street
New York, NY 10013
T 212 226 8413

**Campbell Apartment** [66]
Grand Central Station
87 East 42nd Street
New York, NY 10017
T 212 953 0409
W www.
grandcentralterminal.com

**Castor & Pollux** [174]
238 West 10th Street
New York, NY 10014
T 212 645 6572
E ladies@
castorandpolluxstore.com
W www.
castorandpolluxstore.com

**Chanterelle** [16]
2 Harrison Street
New York, NY 10013
T 212 966 6960
E inq@chanterellenyc.com
W www.chanterellenyc.com

**Char No. 4** [157]
196 Smith Street

Brooklyn, NY 11201
T 718 643 2106

**Chelsea Market** [36]
75 Ninth Avenue
New York, NY 10011
W www.chelseamarket.com

**ChikaLicious** [54]
203 East 10th Street
New York, NY 10003
T 212 995 9511
E info@chikalicious.com
W www.chikalicious.com

**Chrysler Building** [68]
405 Lexington Avenue
New York, NY 10036
T 212 682 3070

**Cielo** [42]
18 Little West 12th Street
New York, NY 10014
T 212 645 5700
W www.cieloclub.com

**City Bakery** [53]
3 West 18th Street
New York, NY 10011
T 212 366 1414
W www.thecitybakery.com

**City Club Hotel** [118]
55 West 44th Street
New York, NY 10036
T 212 921 5500
W www.cityclubhotel.com

**C.O. Bigelow
Apothecaries** [46]
414 Sixth Avenue
New York, NY 10011
T 212 533 2700
W www.bigelowchemists.com

**Comme des Garçons** [41]
520 West 22nd Street
New York, NY 10011
T 212 604 9200

**Commissary** [81]
1030 Third Avenue
New York, NY 10021
T 212 339 9955

**Conservatory Garden** [85]
Central Park
Fifth Avenue at East 105th Street
New York, NY 10029
W www.centralpark.org

**Cooper-Hewitt National
Design Museum** [82]
2 East 91st Street
New York, NY 10128
T 212 849 8400
W www.ndm.si.edu

**Corner Bistro** [140]
331 West 4th Street
New York, NY 10014
T 212 242 9502

**Deadly Dragon Sound System** [60]
102b Forsyth Street
New York, NY 10002
T  646 613 0139
E  info@deadlydragonsound.com
W  www.deadlydragonsound.com

**Decibel** [55]
240 East 9th Street
New York 10003
T  212 979 2733

**Deitch Projects** [25]
76 Grand Street
New York, NY 10013
T  212 343 7300
18 Wooster Street
New York, NY 10013
T  212 941 9475
E  info@deitch.com
W  www.deitch.com

**Delicatessen** [26]
54 Prince Street
New York, NY 10012
T  212 226 0211
E  info@delicatessennyc.com
W  www.delicatessennyc.com

**DIA Center for the Arts** [39]
535 West 22nd Street
New York, NY 10011
T  212 989 5566
E  info@diaart.org
W  www.diacenter.org

**Diane von Furstenberg** [46]
874 Washington Street
New York, NY 10014
T  646 486 4800
W  www.dvf.com

**Diner** [138]
85 Broadway
Brooklyn, NY 11211
T  718 486 3077
E  dinercontact@dinernyc.com
W  www.dinernyc.com

**Donald Judd House** [25]
101 Spring Street
New York, NY 10012
T  212 219 2747
E  info@juddfoundation.org
W  www.juddfoundation.org

**Doughnut Plant** [58]
379 Grand Street
New York, NY 10002
T  212 505 3700
W  www.doughnutplant.com

**Dovetail** [86]
103 West 77th Street
New York, NY 10024
T  212 362 3800
E  info@dovetailnyc.com
W  www.dovetailnyc.com

**Dressler** [99]
149 Broadway
Brooklyn, NY 11211

T  718 384 6343
W  www.dresslernyc.com

**Duane Park** [16]
Duane and Hudson Streets
New York, NY 10013
W  www.duanepark.org

**Dumpling House** [58]
118 Eldridge Street
New York, NY 10002
T  212 625 8008

**Economy Candy** [56]
108 Rivington Street
New York, NY 10002
T  800 352 4544
W  www.economycandy.com

**Egg** [95]
135 North 5th Street
Brooklyn, NY 11211
T  718 302 5151
E  info@pigandegg.com
W  www.pigandegg.com

**El Quijote** [41]
226 West 23rd Street
New York, NY 10011
T  212 929 1855
W  www.elquijoterestaurant.com

**Fanelli's** [25]
94 Prince Street
New York, NY 10012
T  212 226 9412

**Fette Sau** [139]
354 Metropolitan Avenue
Brooklyn, NY 11211
T  718 963 3404

**Flight 001** [46]
96 Greenwich Avenue
New York, NY 10011
T  212 989 0001
E  info@flight001.com
W  www.flight001.com

**Four Seasons Bar** [159]
Seagram Building
99 East 52nd Street
New York, NY 10022
T  212 754 9494
W  www.fourseasons
   restaurant.com

**Frankie's Spuntino** [58]
17 Clinton Street
New York, NY 10002
T  212 253 2303
E  info@frankiesspuntino.com
W  www.frankiesspuntino.com

**Frank's Cocktail Lounge** [109]
660 Fulton Street
Brooklyn, NY 11238
T  718 625 9339
E  trumaster1@aol.com
W  www.
   frankscocktaillounge.com

**Fraunces Tavern** [60]
54 Pearl Street
New York, NY 10004
T  212 968 1776
W  www.frauncestavern.com

**Freeman's** [137]
2 Freeman Alley
New York, NY 10002
T  212 420 0012
E  info@freemansrestaurant.com
W  www.freemansrestaurant.com

**Frick Collection** [81]
1 East 70th Street
New York, NY 10021
T  212 288 0700
E  info@frick.org
W  www.frick.org

**Future Perfect** [166]
115 North 6th Street
Brooklyn, NY 11211
T  718 599 6278
E  hello@thefutureperfect.com
W  www.thefutureperfect.com

**Gagosian Gallery** [35]
555 West 24th Street
New York, NY 10011
T  212 741 1111
E  newyork@gagosian.com
W  www.gagosian.com

**Gavin Brown's Enterprise** [17]
620 Greenwich Street
New York, NY 10014
T  212 627 5258
E  gallery@gavinbrown.biz
W  www.gavinbrown.biz

**Gladstone Gallery** [36]
515 West 24th Street
New York, NY 10011
T  212 206 9300
530 West 21st Street
New York, NY 10011
T  212 206 7606
E  info@gladstonegallery.com
W  www.gladstonegallery.com

**Glasslands Gallery** [95]
289 Kent Avenue
Brooklyn, NY 11211
E  theglasslands@gmail.com
W  www.glasslands.com

**Gramercy Tavern** [53]
42 East 20th Street
New York, NY 10003
T  212 477 0777
E  info@gramercytavern.com
W  www.gramercytavern.com

**Grand Central Oyster Bar & Restaurant** [141]
Grand Central Station
87 East 42nd Street
New York, NY 10017
T  212 490 6650
W  www.oysterbarny.com

**Grand Central Station** [66]
87 East 42nd Street
New York, NY 10017
W  www.
   grandcentralterminal.com

**Great NY Noodletown** [18]
28 1/2 Bowery
New York, NY 10013
T  212 349 0923

**Greenmarket** [54]
Union Square
East 17th Street and Broadway
New York, NY 10003
T  212 788 7476
W  www.cenyc.org

**Greenwich Hotel** [116]
377 Greenwich Street
New York, NY 10013
T  212 941 8900
E  info@thegreenwichhotel.com
W  www.thegreenwichhotel.com

**Guastavino's** [82]
409 East 59th Street
New York, NY 10022
T  212 980 2711
E  arelucio@guastavinos.com
W  www.guastavinos.com

**Guggenheim Museum** [85]
1071 Fifth Avenue
New York, NY 10128
T  212 423 3618
E  visitorinfo@guggenheim.org
W  www.guggenheim.org

**Hannah Clark** [164]
60 East 4th Street
New York, NY 10003
T  212 539 1970
E  info@hannah-clark.com
W  www.hannah-clark.com

**Helmut Lang Parfumerie** [26]
81 Greene Street
New York, NY 10012
T  212 334 3921
W  www.helmutlang.com

**High Line Park** [41]
529 West 20th Street, Suite 8W
New York, NY 10011
T  212 206 9922
E  info@thehighline.org
W  www.thehighline.org

**Hotel Chelsea** [128]
222 West 23rd Street
New York, NY 10011
T  212 243 3700
E  reservations@
   hotelchelsea.com
W  www.hotelchelsea.com

**Hotel on Rivington** [132]
107 Rivington Street
New York, NY 10002
T  212 475 2600

E info@
hotelonrivington.com
W www.hotelonrivington.com

**I Heart** [163]
262 Mott Street
New York, NY 10012
T 212 219 9265

**Isamu Noguchi Garden Museum** [99]
9–01 33rd Road
Long Island City, NY 11106
T 718 204 7088
E info@noguchi.org
W www.noguchi.org

**Jack Spade** [170]
56 Greene Street
New York, NY 10012
T 212 625 1820
E customerservice@
jackspade.com
W www.jackspade.com

**Jacques Torres** [100]
66 Water Street
Brooklyn, NY 11201
T 212 414 2462
E info@mrchocolate.com
W www.jacquestorres.com

**Jeffrey** [45]
449 West 14th Street
New York, NY 10014
T 212 206 1272
W www.jeffreynewyork.com

**Jen Bekman** [21]
6 Spring Street
New York, NY 10012
T 212 219 0166
E info@jenbekman.com
W www.jenbekman.com

**Joe's Dairy** [26]
156 Sullivan Street
New York, NY 10012
T 212 677 8780

**Joe's Pub** [29]
425 Lafayette Street
New York, NY 10003
T 212 539 8778
E info@joespub.com
W www.joespub.com

**Junior's** [109]
386 Flatbush Avenue
Brooklyn, NY 11201
T 718 852 5257
E info@juniorscheesecake.com
W www.juniorscheesecake.com

**Katz's Delicatessen** [145]
205 East Houston Street
New York, NY 10002
T 212 254 2246
E info@katzdeli.com
W www.katzdeli.com

**Kidrobot** [25]
118 Prince Street

New York, NY 10012
T 212 966 6688
E nystore@kidrobot.com
W www.kidrobot.com

**Kiehl's** [169]
109 Third Avenue
New York, NY 10003
T 212 677 3171
W www.kiehls.com

**King Cole Bar** [155]
St. Regis Hotel
2 East 55th Street
New York, NY 10022
T 212 753 4500
W www.starwoodhotels.com/
stregis

**Kinokuniya** [74]
1073 Avenue of the Americas
New York, NY 10018
T 212 869 1700
E nyinfo@kinokuniya.com
W www.kinokuniya.com

**Kirna Zabête** [164]
96 Greene Street
New York, NY 10012
T 212 941 9656
W www.kirnazabete.com

**La Esquina** [21]
114 Kenmare Street
New York, NY 10012
T 646 613 7100
W www.esquinanyc.com

**La Lunchonette** [42]
130 Tenth Avenue
New York, NY 10011
T 212 675 0342

**Layla** [106]
86 Hoyt Street
Brooklyn, NY 11201
T 718 222 1933
E info@layla-bklyn.com
W www.layla-bklyn.com

**Le Cirque** [142]
1 Beacon Court
151 East 58th Street
New York, NY 10022
T 212 644 0202
W www.lecirque.com

**Lenox Lounge** [88]
288 Lenox Avenue
(Malcolm X Boulevard)
New York, NY 10027
T 212 427 0253
E info@lenoxlounge.com
W www.lenoxlounge.com

**Lever House Restaurant** [143]
390 Park Avenue
New York, NY 10022
T 212 888 2700
W www.leverhouse.com

**Lincoln Center for the Performing Arts** [86]
70 Lincoln Center Plaza
New York, NY 10023
T 212 875 5456
E customerservice@
lincolncenter.org
W www.lincolncenter.org

**Linda Dresner** [71]
484 Park Avenue
New York, NY 10022
T 212 308 3177
E infony@lindadresner.com
W www.lindadresner.com

**Liz Christy Garden** [29]
East Houston Street, between
Second Avenue and Bowery
New York, NY 10013
E dlogg60798@aol.com
W www.lizchristygarden.org

**Louis Vuitton** [71]
1 East 57th Street
New York, NY 10022
T 212 758 8877
W www.vuitton.com

**Lower East Side Tenement Museum** [58]
97 Orchard Street
New York, NY 10002
T 212 982 8420
E lestm@tenement.org
W www.tenement.org

**Luhring Augustine** [36]
531 West 24th Street
New York, NY 10011
T 212 206 9100
E info@luhringaugustine.com
W www.luhringaugustine.com

**Lure Fish Bar** [146]
142 Mercer Street
New York, NY 10012
T 212 431 7676
E info@lurefishbar.com
W www.lurefishbar.com

**Lyell** [21]
173 Elizabeth Street
New York, NY 10012
T 212 966 8484
E newyork@lyellnyc.com
W www.lyellnyc.com

**Magnolia Bakery** [45]
401 Bleecker Street
New York, NY 10014
T 212 462 2572
E info@magnoliabakery.com
W www.magnoliacupcakes.com

**Malin + Goetz** [41]
177 Seventh Avenue
New York, NY 10011
T 212 727 3777
E info@malinandgoetz.com
W www.malinandgoetz.com

**Marc Jacobs** [172]
385 Bleecker Street
New York, NY 10014
T 212 924 6126
403–5 Bleecker Street
New York, NY 10014
T 212 924 0026
163 Mercer Street
New York, NY 10012
T 212 343 1490
W www.marcjacobs.com

**Mary's Fish Camp** [46]
64 Charles Street
New York, NY 10014
T 646 486 2185
W www.marysfishcamp.com

**Matthew Marks Gallery** [36]
523 West 24th Street
New York, NY 10011
T 212 243 0200
E info@matthewmarks.com
W www.matthewmarks.com

**Maxilla and Mandible** [85]
451 Columbus Avenue
New York, NY 10024
T 212 724 6173
E maxilla@maxillaand
mandible.com
W www.maxillaand
mandible.com

**Max Protetch Gallery** [39]
511 West 22nd Street
New York, NY 10011
T 212 633 6999
E info@maxprotetch.com
W www.maxprotetch.com

**Mayle** [173]
252 Elizabeth Street
New York, NY 10012
T 212 625 0406
E mayleorder@mayleonline.com
W www.mayleonline.com

**McSorley's Old Ale House** [151]
15 East 7th Street
New York, NY 10003
T 212 474 9148
W www.mcsorleysnewyork.com

**Me & Ro** [169]
241 Elizabeth Street
New York, NY 10012
T 917 237 9215
E meandrony@
meandrojewelry.com
W www.meandrojewelry.com

**Megu** [140]
62 Thomas Street
New York, NY 10013
T 212 964 7777
W www.megunyc.com

**Merc Bar** [25]
151 Mercer Street
New York, NY 10012
T 212 966 2727

E   info@mercbar.com
W   www.mercbar.com

**Mercedes-Benz
Showroom** [71]
430 Park Avenue
New York, NY 10022
T   212 629 1492
E   daniel.siegel@mbusa.com
W   www.mb-manhattan.com

**Merchant's House
Museum** [29]
29 East 4th Street
New York, NY 10003
T   212 777 1089
E   nyc1832@
    merchantshouse.com
W   www.merchantshouse.com

**Metropolitan Museum
of Art** [82]
**Iris and B. Gerald Cantor
Roof Garden** [82]
1000 Fifth Avenue
New York, NY 10028
T   212 535 7710
W   www.metmuseum.org

**Mies Design Shop** [74]
319 West 47th Street
New York, NY 10036
T   212 247 3132

**MoMA Design and Book
Store** [175]
11 West 53rd Street
New York, NY 10019
T   212 708 9700
E   feedback@moma.org
W   www.momastore.org

**Momenta Art** [95]
359 Bedford Avenue
Brooklyn, NY 11211
T   718 218 8058
W   www.momentaart.org

**Momofuku Ssäm Bar** [144]
207 Second Avenue
New York, NY 10003
T   212 254 3500
W   www.momofuku.com

**Morgan Library** [66]
225 Madison Avenue
New York, NY 10016
T   212 685 0008
E   visitorservices@
    themorgan.org
W   www.themorgan.org

**Moss** [167]
150 Greene Street
New York, NY 10012
T   212 204 7100
E   store@mossonline.com
W   www.mossonline.com

**Moto** [96]
394 Broadway
Brooklyn, NY 11211

T   718 599 6895
W   www.circa1938.com

**Museum of Arts
and Design** [74]
2 Columbus Circle
New York, NY 10019
T   212 299 7777
E   info@madmuseum.org
W   www.madmuseum.org

**Museum of Modern Art** [67]
11 West 53rd Street
New York, NY 10019
T   212 708 9400
E   info@moma.org
W   www.moma.org

**National Arts Club** [53]
15 Gramercy Park South
New York, NY 10003
T   212 475 3424
W   www.nationalartsclub.org

**Neue Galerie** [85]
1048 Fifth Avenue
New York, NY 10028
T   212 628 6200
E   museum@neuegalerie.org
W   www.neuegalerie.org

**New Museum** [55]
235 Bowery
New York, NY 10002
T   212 219 1222
E   info@newmuseum.org
W   www.newmuseum.org

**New York Public
Library** [68]
Fifth Avenue at 42nd Street
New York, NY 10018
T   212 930 0800
W   www.nypl.org

**New York Stock
Exchange** [60]
8 Broad Street
New York, NY 10005
T   212 656 3000
W   www.nyse.com

**New York Times
Building** [71]
620 Eighth Avenue
New York, NY 10017
W   www.
    newyorktimesbuilding.com

**Nom de Guerre** [29]
640 Broadway, Lower Level
New York, NY 10012
T   212 253 2891
E   info@nomdeguerre.net
W   www.nomdeguerre.net

**Odeon** [141]
145 West Broadway
New York, NY 10013
T   212 233 0507
W   www.theodeonrestaurant.com

**Opening Ceremony** [18]
33 Howard Street
New York, NY 10013
T   212 219 2688
E   purple@openingceremony.us
W   www.openingceremony.us

**Other Music** [29]
15 East 4th Street
New York, NY 10003
T   212 477 8150
E   sales@othermusic.com
W   www.othermusic.com

**Paley Park** [67]
East 53rd Street, between
Madison and Fifth Avenues
New York, NY 10022

**Pastis** [44]
9 Ninth Avenue
New York, NY 10014
T   212 929 4844
W   www.pastisny.com

**PDT** [155]
113 St. Mark's Place
New York, NY 10009
T   212 614 0386

**Peasant Wine Bar** [18]
194 Elizabeth Street
New York, NY 10012
T   212 965 9511
E   info@peasantnyc.com
W   www.peasantnyc.com

**Pete's Candy Store** [95]
709 Lorimer Street
Brooklyn, NY 11211
T   718 302 3770
E   andy@petescandystore.com
W   www.petescandystore.com

**Pete's Tavern** [53]
129 East 18th Street
New York, NY 10003
T   212 473 7676
E   garyeagan@hotmail.com
W   www.petestavern.com

**Pierogi 2000** [95]
177 North 9th Street
Brooklyn, NY 11211
T   718 599 2144
E   info@pierogi2000.com
W   www.pierogi2000.com

**Prada** [170]
575 Broadway
New York, NY 10012
T   212 334 8888
W   www.prada.com

**Printed Matter** [38]
195 Tenth Avenue
New York, NY 10011
T   212 925 0325
W   www.printedmatter.org

**Project No. 8** [165]
138 Division Street
New York, NY 10002

T   212 925 5599
E   info@projectno8.com
W   www.projectno8.com

**P.S.1 Contemporary
Art Center** [100]
22–25 Jackson Avenue
Long Island City, NY 11101
T   718 784 2084
E   mail@ps1.org
W   www.ps1.org

**Public** [147]
210 Elizabeth Street
New York, NY 10012
T   212 343 7011
E   info@public-nyc.com
W   www.public-nyc.com

**Radegast** [96]
113 North 3rd Street
Brooklyn, NY 11211
T   718 963 3973
W   www.radegasthall.com

**Rag & Bone** [46]
100 and 104 Christopher Street
New York, NY 10014
T   212 727 2990
E   info@rag-bone.com
W   www.rag-bone.com

**Ralph Lauren** [81]
867 Madison Avenue
New York, NY 10021
T   212 606 2100
W   www.ralphlauren.com

**Red Flower** [26]
13 Prince Street
New York, NY 10012
T   212 966 5301
E   13prince@redflower.com
W   www.redflower.com

**Roosevelt Island
Tramway** [82]
59th Street at Second Avenue
T   212 832 4555
E   information@rioc.org
W   www.rioc.org

**Russ & Daughters** [56]
179 East Houston Street
New York, NY 10002
T   212 475 4880
E   info@russanddaughters.com
W   www.russanddaughters.com

**Russian Samovar** [73]
256 West 52nd Street
New York, NY 10019
T   212 757 0168
E   info@russiansamovar.com
W   www.russiansamovar.com

**St. Mark's Bookshop** [54]
31 Third Avenue
New York, NY 10003
T   212 260 7853
E   stmarksbooks@
    mindspring.com
W   www.stmarksbookshop.com

**Santos Party House** [18]
96 Lafayette Street
New York, NY 10013
T   212 714 4646
W   www.santospartyhouse.com

**Scarpetta** [35]
355 West 14th Street
New York, NY 10014
T   212 691 0555
E   info@scarpettanyc.com
W   www.scarpettanyc.com

**Schiller's Liquor Bar** [56]
131 Rivington Street
New York, NY 10002
T   212 260 4555
E   info@schillersny.com
W   www.schillersny.com

**SculptureCenter** [100]
44–19 Purves Street
Long Island City, NY 11101
T   718 361 1750
E   info@sculpture-center.org
W   www.sculpture-center.org

**Seize Sur Vingt** [171]
243 Elizabeth Street
New York, NY 10012
T   212 343 0476
E   nyc@16sur20.com
W   www.16sur20.com

**Seventh Regiment
Armory** [82]
643 Park Avenue
New York, NY 10065
T   212 616 3930
E   info@armoryonpark.org
W   www.armoryonpark.org

**Sherwood Café at
Robin des Bois** [153]
195 Smith Street
Brooklyn, NY 11201
T   718 596 1609
W   www.sherwoodcafe.com

**Sigerson Morrison** [163]
28 Prince Street
New York, NY 11012
T   212 625 1641
W   www.sigersonmorrison.com

**Skyscraper Museum** [60]
39 Battery Place
New York, NY 10280
T   212 968 1961
W   www.skyscraper.org

**Socrates Sculpture
Park** [99]
Broadway and Vernon Boulevard
Long Island City, NY 11106
T   718 956 1819
E   info@
   socratessculpturepark.org
W   www.
   socratessculpturepark.org

**Spoonbill & Sugartown** [96]
218 Bedford Avenue

Brooklyn, NY 11211
T   718 387 7322
E   sugar@spoonbillbooks.com
W   www.spoonbillbooks.com

**Spotted Pig** [44]
314 West 11th Street
New York, NY 10014
T   212 620 0393
E   info@thespottedpig.com
W   www.thespottedpig.com

**Spring** [100]
126a Front Street
Brooklyn, NY 11201
T   718 222 1054
W   www.spring3d.net

**Starrett Lehigh
Building** [36]
601 West 26th Street
New York, NY 10001
T   212 924 0505
E   pthorsen@601west.com
W   www.starrett-
   lehighbuilding.com

**Steinway & Sons** [74]
109 West 57th Street
New York, NY 10019
T   212 246 1100
E   showrooms@steinway.com
W   www.steinway.com

**Steven Alan** [175]
103 Franklin Street
New York, NY 10013
T   212 343 0352
E   orders@stevenalan.com
W   www.stevenalan.com

**Steven Salen Tailors** [68]
18 East 53rd Street
New York, NY 10022
T   212 755 5665

**Storefront for Art
and Architecture** [18]
97 Kenmare Street
New York, NY 10012
T   212 431 5795
E   info@storefrontnews.org
W   www.storefrontnews.org

**Studio Museum
in Harlem** [88]
144 West 125th Street (Dr. Martin
Luther King, Jr. Boulevard)
New York, NY 10027
T   212 864 4500
W   www.studiomuseum.org

**Sylvia's Soul Food
Restaurant** [88]
328 Lenox Avenue
(Malcolm X Boulevard)
New York, NY 10027
T   212 996 0660
E   info@sylviasrestaurant.com
W   www.sylviassoulfood.com

**Tabla** [53]
11 Madison Avenue

New York, NY 10010
T   212 889 0667
E   tcoughlin@tablany.com
W   www.tablany.com

**Takashimaya** [72]
693 Fifth Avenue
New York, NY 10022
T   212 350 0100
W   www.ny-takashimaya.com

**Ted Muehling** [22]
27 Howard Street
New York, NY 10013
T   212 431 3825
E   tmuehling@gmail.com
W   www.tedmuehling.com

**Temple Bar** [159]
332 Lafayette Street
New York, NY 10012
T   212 925 4242
W   www.templebarnyc.com

**TG170** [58]
170 Ludlow Street
New York, NY 10002
T   212 995 8660
E   info@tg170.com
W   www.tg170.com

**The Broken Kilometer** [26]
393 West Broadway
New York, NY 10012
W   www.brokenkilometer.org

**The Inn at Irving Place** [120]
56 Irving Place
New York, NY 10003
T   212 533 4600
E   innatirving@aol.com
W   www.innatirving.com

**The Jane** [124]
113 Jane Street
New York, NY 10014
T   212 924 6700
E   reservations@thejanenyc.com
W   www.thejanenyc.com

**The Kitchen** [41]
512 West 19th Street
New York, NY 10011
T   212 255 5793
E   info@thekitchen.org
W   www.thekitchen.org

**The Lowell** [126]
28 East 63rd Street
New York, NY 10065
T   212 838 1400
E   reservations@lowellhotel.com
W   www.lowellhotel.com

**The New York
Earth Room** [26]
141 Wooster Street
New York, NY 10012
W   www.earthroom.org

**The New York
Shaving Company** [21]
202b Elizabeth Street

New York, NY 10012
T   212 334 9495
E   elizabethstreet@
   theshaveofnewyork.com
W   www.theshaveofnewyork.com

**The Park** [152]
118 Tenth Avenue
New York, NY 10011
T   212 352 3313
W   www.theparknyc.com

**The Red Cat** [42]
227 Tenth Avenue
New York, NY 10011
T   212 242 1122
W   www.theredcat.com

**The Rusty Knot** [154]
425 West Street
New York, NY 10014
T   212 645 5668
E   therustyknot@gmail.com

**Thomas Beisl** [109]
25 Lafayette Avenue
Brooklyn, NY 11217
T   718 222 5800

**Thompson
Lower East Side** [122]
190 Allen Street
New York, NY 10002
T   212 460 5300
E   infoles@thompsonhotels.com
W   www.thompsonles.com

**Tía Pol** [41]
205 Tenth Avenue
New York, NY 10011
T   212 675 8805
W   www.tiapol.com

**Tiffany's** [71]
Fifth Avenue at 57th Street
New York, NY 10022
T   212 755 8000
W   www.tiffany.com

**Times Square** [74]
Broadway and Seventh Avenue,
between West 42nd and
West 47th Streets
New York, NY 10036
E   info@timessquarealliance.org
W   www.timessquarenyc.org

**Tompkins Square Park** [56]
Avenues A to B, and East 7th to
East 10th Streets
New York, NY 10009
W   www.nycgovparks.org

**Tribeca Issey Miyake** [17]
119 Hudson Street
New York, NY 10013
T   212 226 0100
E   info@tribecaisseymiyake.com
W   www.tribecaisseymiyake.com

**Unis** [21]
226 Elizabeth Street
New York, NY 10012

T 212 431 5533
E info@unisnewyork.com
W www.unisnewyork.com

**United Nations Headquarters** [68]
First Avenue at 46th Street
New York, NY 10017
T 212 963 8687
E toursunhq@un.org
W www.un.org/tours

**Ursus Rare Books** [82]
Carlyle Hotel
981 Madison Avenue
New York, NY 10075
T 212 772 8787
E ursus@ursusbooks.com
W www.ursusbooks.com

**Vinegar Hill House** [100]
72 Hudson Avenue
Brooklyn, NY 11201
T 718 522 1018
E info@vinegarhillhouse.com
W www.vinegarhillhouse.com

**Visionaire** [22]
11 Mercer Street
New York, NY 10013
T 212 274 8959
E info@visionaireworld.com
W www.visionaireworld.com

**Vitra Showroom** [46]
29 Ninth Avenue
New York, NY 10014
T 212 463 5700
W www.vitra.com

**Watts on Smith** [106]
248 Smith Street
Brooklyn, NY 11231
T 718 596 2359
E info@wattsonsmith.com
W www.wattsonsmith.com

**WD–50** [58]
50 Clinton Street
New York, NY 10002
T 212 477 2900
W www.wd-50.com

**Zabar's** [86]
2245 Broadway
New York, NY 10024
T 212 787 2000
E info@zabars.com
W www.zabars.com

**Zakka** [100]
155 Plymouth Street
Brooklyn, NY 11201
T 718 801 8037
E info@zakkacorp.com
W www.zakkacorp.com

**Ziegfeld Theater** [74]
141 West 54th Street
New York, NY 10019
T 212 307 1862
W www.clearviewcinemas.com

**BUCKS COUNTY** [180]
*If you are not driving, take the bus from Port Authority to Doylestown, Pennsylvania. Bus schedules can be found at www.transbridgebus.com*

Fonthill
East Court Street and Route 313
Doylestown, PA 18901
T 215 348 9461
E fhmail@fonthillmuseum.org
W www.mercermuseum.org/fonthill
*Monday–Saturday 10am–5pm
Sunday 12pm–5pm*

Mercer Museum
84 South Pine Street
Doylestown, PA 18901
T 215 345 0210
F 215 230 0823
E info@mercermuseum.org
W www.mercermuseum.org
*Monday–Saturday 10am–5pm
Tuesday 10am–9pm
Sunday 12pm–5pm*

**CATSKILLS** [178]
*Saugerties does not have a train station, but from Penn Station you can take the Amtrak rail line to Rhinecliff (15 miles to the east of Saugerties) or from Grand Central Station the MetroNorth rail service to Poughkeepsie, and then get a taxi to Saugerties. By car, the drive takes an hour and forty-five minutes up the west side of the Hudson River along the Palisades Parkway and then the New York State Thruway North (I-87). The Villa at Saugerties is a couple of miles outside the town. For detailed directions, see their website.*

Storm King Art Center
Old Pleasant Hill Road
Mountainville, NY 10953
T 845 534 3115
W www.stormking.org
*Open April-October,
Wednesday-Sunday 11am-5:30pm*

Café Tamayo
89 Partition Street
Saugerties, NY 12477
T 845 246 9371
W www.cafetamayo.com

The Villa at Saugerties
159 Fawn Road
Saugerties, NY 12477
T 845 246 0682
E upstatevilla@aol.com
W www.thevillaatsaugerties.com
Rooms from $145

Golden Nugget Antique Flea Market
1850 River Road
Lambertville, NJ 08530
T 609 397 0811

E info@gnmarket.com
W www.gnmarket.com
*Wednesday, Saturday, and Sunday 6am–4pm*

Lambertville Antique Flea Market
1864 River Road
Lambertville, NJ 08530
T 609 397 0456
*Wednesday, Saturday, and Sunday 8am–4pm*

**EAST HAMPTON** [184]
*By car, take the I-27 along the south fork of Long Island to Bridgehampton and East Hampton. For Shelter Island, take the ferry from Sag Harbor. The train journey from Penn Station to East Hampton on the LIRR takes about two and a half hours; further information is available by calling 718 217 5477. You can also take the Hampton Jitney bus; information and details on 631 283 4600 or 800 936 0440.*

Glen Horowitz Bookseller
87 Newtown Lane
East Hampton, NY 11937
T 631 324 5511
E info@ghbookseller.com
W www.ghbookseller.com
*Monday–Saturday 10am–5pm
Sunday 12pm–4pm
Closed Wednesday and Thursday,
October–April*

Pollock-Krasner House
830 Fireplace Road
East Hampton, NY 11937
T 631 324 4929
E hharrison@notes.cc.sunysb.edu
W http://naples.cc.sunysb.edu/cas/pkhouse.nsf
*Open May–October
Thursday, Friday, and Saturday*

Dan Flavin Art Institute
Corwith Avenue off Main Street
Bridgehampton, NY 11932
T 631 537 1476
E info@diaart.org
W www.diacenter.org/ltproj/flavbrid

Sunset Beach Hotel
35 Shore Road
Shelter Island, NY 11965
T 631 749 2001
E reservations@sunsetbeachli.com
W www.sunsetbeachli.com
Rooms from $245

1770 House
143 Main Street
East Hampton, NY 11937
T 631 324 1770
E innkeeper@1770house.com
W www.1770house.com
Rooms from $295

**HUDSON RIVER VALLEY** [182]
*Take the MetroNorth rail service from Grand Central Station to Beacon, and then one stop back toward New York to Cold Spring. By car, take the Palisades Parkway North, cross Bear Mountain Bridge and take Route 9D north to Beacon. The journey is approximately 90 minutes.*

Dia:Beacon
3 Beekman Street
Beacon, NY 12508
T 845 440 0100
E info@diabeacon.org
W www.diabeacon.org

Pig Hill Inn
73 Main Street
Cold Spring, NY 10516
T 845 265 9247
E pighillinn@aol.com
W www.pighillinn.com
Rooms from $150

East Side Kitchen
124 Main Street
Cold Spring, NY 10516
T 845 265 7223
*Closed Mondays*